BUNGALOW COLORS

EXTERIORS

BUNGALOW COLORS EXTERIORS

ROBERT SCHWEITZER

Gibbs Smith, Publisher
Salt Lake City

First Edition
06 05 04   5 4

Text © 2002 by Robert Schweitzer
Photographs on pages 2, 18, 26, 30–31, 86, 112, 114–115, 192 © Linda Svendsen
Photograph on pages 8–9 courtesy of The Bungalow Company
All other photographs © Robert Schweitzer unless otherwise noted

Published by
Gibbs Smith, Publisher
P.O. Box 667
Layton, Utah 84041

Orders: (800) 748-5439
www.gibbs-smith.com

Edited by Monica Millward Weeks
Designed and produced by Woodland Studio
Printed in Hong Kong

Library of Congress Cataloging-in-Publication Data

Schweitzer, Robert, 1949-
  Bungalow colors : exteriors / Robert Schweitzer.— 1st ed.
    p. cm.
  ISBN 1-58685-130-6
  1. Bungalows—United States. 2. Color in architecture—United States.
  3. Arts and crafts movement—United States. I. Title.
  NA7571 .S39 2002
  728'.373'0973—dc21
                        2002001152

CONTENTS

ACKNOWLEDGMENTS

Special thanks to Professor Kingsbury Marzolf, who started me along the architectural history road almost thirty years ago. Marshall McLennan and Ted Ligibel deserve thanks for allowing me to teach in their fine Historic Preservation program for more than twenty years. Also important are all my graduate students from Eastern Michigan University.

Special people deserving of thanks include the following:

Greg Slater, for his work on Baillie Scott

The Bungalow Company

Ken Haines (The Color Wheel Company)

Sharon Ferraro, for her research on the *Ladies' Home Journal* homes

Carol Kamm of the Arts & Crafts Society, for her work on my Web site and for being
    a generally neat person

Roger Moss, for his pioneering work on exterior colors

John Crosby Freeman, for his research on historic colors

John Brinkmann (*American Bungalow* magazine)

Erika Kotite (*Victorian Homes* magazine)

Thanks are due to the following homeowners who supplied photographs of their homes:

Nick Stearns

Michael and Kimberly Hoyt

Shelley and Griff Hearn

Gerald Duprey and Mark Uhen

Mike and Kimberly Shinnebarger

Susan Rathkey

Susan and Brian Kuhawski

Lesha and Samuel Greengus

Nancy Stumpp, Corporation for Environmental Management

Ann and Kip Bonds

Douglas Romary

Sari Kalin and Michael Ricciuti

Mark Bowie

Ethan and Cheryl Lewis

Don and Sharon Reinhard

Sharon Stroble

Beth Hawkins

Shirley Hyatt and Terry Miller

Sandra Tomita and Larry Berkowitz

Sharon Linstedt and Mark Mahoney

Jori and Robert Owens

John and Mona Fandel

Marc and Christianna Mosley

Beverly and Timothy Miller

Patti LeCraft

Ed and Randi Peterson

Janelle and Erik Johannesen

Patrick and Theresa Whaley

Susan Ruth and Ben Rodriquez

Jeff Engler

Karen and Kevin McClusker

Rhiannon Allen

Monica Weeks and Marty Lee at Gibbs Smith, Publisher, for their help and encouragement.

More than all others, daughters Teagan and Elsbeth are special for their encouragement and love. My wife, Glenna, is exceptional for all her years of support and the special work on the Color Theory chapter. Good buddy Al (the fox terrier) is thanked for keeping out of the piles of paper littering the house.

INTRODUCTION

At the turn of the twenty-first century an incredible interest in the early years of the twentieth century and its corresponding Arts & Crafts design philosophy has surfaced. Television programs devoted to showcasing Craftsman and Bungalow homes appear weekly. Several popular magazines written entirely on the topic of restoring and decorating homes in the Arts & Crafts style are currently in print. New subdivisions of "modern bungalows" are springing up all across the nation. Yet, surprisingly enough, not one book is available on how to go about selecting exterior colors for the historic or newly built bungalow. This work is an attempt to bring together the various elements that are necessary to undertake the task of designing an exterior color scheme and bring it to completion.

The sections that follow start out by providing some important historical background about the homes of the early twentieth century, where their design inspirations came from, and why they look the way they do. Next follows useful information on Arts & Crafts home styles of the age and their popular exterior colors, as drawn from actual historic period sources. Some basic color theory follows, explaining why some colors generally work better with others and why some don't. The last sections of the book are devoted to practical application featuring original bungalow period colors directly from early-twentieth-century sources and then providing the steps to create your own bungalow color scheme using modern products. For inspirational purposes, the "Before & After" section illustrates what wonderful transformations can occur through good planning and employing a thoughtful process.

"On entering some of our villages, the only color which meets the eye is white.

. . . Is this taste? Whether it be or not, one thing is certain, that a great change is

coming over our people in this respect. They are beginning to see that there are

beauties in color as well as form."

SAMUEL SLOAN, THE MODERN ARCHITECT, 1852

House Color Changes in the Nineteenth Century

In the early years of the century, house fashion generally favored the Classical Revival style. The architectural elements of Greece and Rome predominated. Houses were typically painted in what was thought at the time to be the style of antiquity—light marble. White and off-white were the most popular colors in use on the house body during the pre–Civil War era. Painters in this period were required to mix their colors on-site in large kettles. This process made white the easiest color to brew consistently between paint batches.

In the 1840s, house designs began to shift to the Gothic Revival and Italianate styles popularized by the published works of Andrew Jackson Downing and Samuel Sloan. These new homes called for updated colors and a movement away from white. Both Downing and Sloan appealed to builders to use more natural colors on the house exterior. They believed that white made the house look stark and not in keeping with the desired naturalistic symbiotic relationship between the house and the landscape. The colors of wood, soil, and rocks were suggested as alternatives. These were known as the "quiet shades" because they were not as stark as white but not a major transition away from it. Writers of this era suggested that when employing these softer colors on the body of the house, the trim and windows of the house should be painted a darker color to avoid monotony.

14

Fig. I. Carrara Paints sample card from the late nineteenth century. These dark shades of the late Victorian Age preceded the Arts & Crafts–period colors and were referred to as the "muddy colors."

After the Civil War, technological advances made major changes possible in not only the architecture of the country but the colors of the buildings as well. With the development and refinement of a new framing technique known as the balloon frame, and the standardization of lumber sizes (the 2 x 4), houses grew in size and complexity. Styles such as the French Mansard, Stick, and Queen Anne became prominent in the 1870s and 1880s. In the paint industry, machinery was developed to grind pigment and mix it into the oil. This improvement resulted in a wider range of more consistent colors. Paint was safely shipped in secure containers via the expanding national rail system, allowing the newest colors to reach homeowners all across America. Advances in the printing industry allowed paint manufacturers to prepare elaborate brochures in color to advertise their new products. The period of the 1870s to the 1890s has been nicknamed the "muddy color" era for its extensive use of dark greens, olives, browns, rusts, and mustard yellows (fig. 1). Because houses were so ornate on the exterior, with wide sweeping verandas and multiple porches bordered with hundreds of wooden spindles, it was suggested by period experts that the homeowner consult with an architect to ensure that the colors applied to the home did not produce a negative effect. Research has shown that homes were painted in five, six, seven, or even nine or more colors. The complexity of the architecture spawned more complex paint schemes. While these late-Victorian-style homes had many opportunities for color placement, it was commonly suggested that the details not be overemphasized by the colors.

As the turn of the century drew closer, house colors began to moderate back to lighter and softer tones. This was particularly due to the introduction of the newest architectural style, Colonial Revival. Beginning in the last quarter of the century, the populace experienced a growing fascination with the nation's early history and particularly the homes of the American colonial period. Their design simplicity and less cluttered look appealed to many people who saw them as a truly American type of building. House bodies began to be painted in softer yellow, light green, and gray tones, with the introduction of white now employed as a trim (fig. 2). The number of colors utilized in the overall color scheme declined as well, with as few as four being common.

Homes took on a softer, almost pastel look, with these new Colonial Revival color schemes. There was not, however, a complete transformation throughout the housing industry.

Fig 2. Georgian Revival–style house in suggested period colors from around the turn of the nineteenth century. The body color is lighter than earlier Victorian color schemes and the formerly dark trim has become white.

Fig. 3. An example of a Colonial Revival–style home in darker Victorian colors. The medium yellow body is framed by heavy dark-green trim. This style of color placement was very popular in the latter part of the 1890s.

Some examples of Colonial Revival homes in darker Victorian colors did exist (fig. 3). House types that were popular in previous decades, such as Queen Anne, continued to be erected well into the twentieth century. They also continued to be painted in darker tones and muddy, grayed colors. As the twentieth century dawned, new design influences from Britain and places as far away as India began to make their presence felt on the American housing scene. These new prototypes introduced new ideas on exterior color.

BRITISH INFLUENCES

"William Morris represents a most important factor in the progress of modern art. He was a member of that group of brilliant, earnest young Englishmen who, at the middle of the Nineteenth Century, revolutionized the national school of painting, and generated a current of aestheticism whose vibrations are still felt, not only in the Parent country, but as well in America and in France.

From his relations with the Pre-Raphaelite Brotherhood and from his own practical genius, Morris evolved a system of household art, which has largely swept away the ugly and the commonplace from the English middle-class home."

GUSTAV STICKLEY, THE CRAFTSMAN, OCTOBER 1901

The popular American housing styles of Bungalow, Craftsman, and Foursquare are all products of the Arts & Crafts movement. To gain an understanding of this movement and its influence on architecture, design, and color, knowledge of the people who precipitated its development is essential.

The roots of what we today call the Arts & Crafts movement took shape in England nearly 170 years ago. British intellectuals recognized that the growing industrialization and the factory system in their nation was causing the degradation of work through the repetition of mindless tasks, the reduction of craft, and the destruction of the environment. In the 1830s and 1840s, men like A. W. N. Pugin began to postulate the foundations of the philosophy that we recognize today as key elements of the Arts & Crafts movement. Pugin rejected popular classical ideals in favor of something he labeled "Medieval Gothicism." He thought the early nineteenth century lacked stability and order, and favored returning to the preindustrial age for artistic inspiration. Pugin believed that the construction of the great cathedrals created the perfect working/craft environment of community of purpose and a "joy of labor." Regarding architecture, Pugin felt that no features on a building should exist that were not necessary. He called for the use of honesty when employing building materials and a respect for the local or vernacular building traditions in any particular region of the country. These ideals were echoed in America seventy years later in the writings and buildings of Frank Lloyd Wright and his Prairie school.

Pugin was the initiator of a philosophy that laid the moral groundwork for the next generation of art reformers such as John Ruskin of Oxford University, who further embellished the ideals. Ruskin lectured and wrote extensively on the need for improved standards of design, for asymmetry and naturalism in art and architecture. In one of his most famous passages, he wrote in *The Seven Lamps of Architecture:*

Gilded Age Houses and Colors

In 1873 Mark Twain published his first novel, one that masterfully captured the spirit of his era. The book's title, *The Gilded Age*, produced a permanent label for the late Victorian period. The post–Civil War period in America fostered the growth of great fortunes, industry, and massive political corruption. It was an age of excess among the moneyed class that witnessed the building of grand manor houses with elaborate decoration on both the interiors and exteriors. The Gilded Age house types of the nineteenth century were diverse, ranging from classical Greek to Gothic, French Mansard to English Queen Anne. Picturesqueness and asymmetry characterized house design. Dwellings acquired towers and turrets and featured a wide variety of wood siding types and colors to adorn them. Some of the houses, because of their ornate wood decoration, were dubbed Bric-a-Brac–style homes.

During the Victorian age in America, the nation's population increased dramatically as European emigration swelled. These new citizens, mostly from central and eastern Europe, were the workers who helped fuel the growing industrial base of the nation. The massive expansion of heavy industry, and a similar growth in the transportation sector, created the need for many new employees across all economic sectors. Cities and smaller towns grew, along with personal income, to a level unknown in the past. This added revenue, coupled with an increase in leisure time, translated into large homes that could accommodate more entertainments and bigger families. Houses also increased in square footage to accommodate space for servants. Both the interior and the exterior of the average house became more complex and more ornate as the century progressed.

His two books *The Seven Lamps of Architecture* (1849) and *The Stones of Venice* (1853) were widely read in the United States towards the end of the nineteenth century. Both Ruskin and Pugin, along with the acknowledged father of the Arts & Crafts movement, William Morris, became the core spokesmen of the British design-reform movement that migrated to American shores in the 1880s. They drew their inspiration from the medieval past rather than the current fashion of copying historical designs. They advocated a simpler lifestyle and thought highly of rural village life. In many ways they were reacting against the industrialization that seemed to limit creativity in art and architecture.

William Morris was a student of Ruskin and went on to become the most famous British Arts & Crafts personality. He put the philosophies of Pugin and Ruskin into practice by starting a commercial decorating firm in 1861. It produced, among many other household items, the celebrated wallpapers with their natural patterns so favored in Arts & Crafts decorating. Morris even carved his own woodblocks to print the wallpaper and developed his own vegetable dyes to color his fabrics. He became well known for his simple marketable style. While devoting a life to the decorative arts, he helped build a movement that has had a lasting effect in Britain and America.

Morris's main goal can be summed up as the desire to bring harmony to the relationship between the designer and the craftsperson, and one way he did this was by establishing craft societies. Morris helped found numerous craft societies in Great Britain in the latter part of the nineteenth century, and those models were copied in the United States to form Arts & Crafts societies in Boston, New York, Chicago, Minneapolis, and Detroit a few years later. The movement was further fueled by the establishment of hundreds more Arts & Crafts groups in the U.S. by 1910. Chicago even boasted its own William Morris Society. Morris helped to set up an interchange of ideas between the British and American Arts & Crafts personalities, groups, and organizations. This Anglo-American cultural exchange included English architect C. R. Ashbee, who visited the States and marveled at the work of the Greene brothers in California and Frank Lloyd Wright in Illinois. Gustav Stickley and Elbert Hubbard, two of the most widely known American promoters of the Arts & Crafts movement, visited England in the 1890s. Magazines and journals on both sides of the Atlantic published articles and pictured works of the most prominent designers and architects.

Morris lectured widely in Britain and collected a circle of friends who formed the core of the maturing English Arts & Crafts movement. Architects like Phillip Webb and painters like Pre-Raphaelites Edward Burne Jones and Dante Gabriel Rossetti helped articulate and promulgate the group's ideals. The Arts & Crafts movement in the 1880s in England was not so much an approach to design or life, but an attitude. While Morris wanted to reform society through enhanced craftsmanship, architects like C. F. A. Voysey wanted to design admirable and more appropriate buildings. He and fellow architects such as C. R. Ashbee and Mackay H. Baillie Scott wanted buildings to be natural and simple, to have order and beauty, and to express the designer's freedom. These ideals were in contrast to the popular and highly ornate Queen Anne Victorian style. Webb designed a house for Morris in this new mode that he christened "Red House" because of its brick color (fig. 4). Built in 1859, it has been acknowledged as the first Arts & Crafts building in Britain. Webb said the house was not designed according to some arbitrary dictate of style, but rather from how the rooms related to each other and how the family would use them. The red brick symbolized the use of natural materials in an honest

Fig. 4. The home of William Morris, English Arts & Crafts leader, at Bexeleyheath in Kent, England. Designed by Phillip Webb in 1859, it is considered the most influential nineteenth-century Arts & Crafts building. (Photo by Kingsbury Marzolf.)

fashion. Morris believed that the house's greatest asset was its unpretentiousness.

British Arts & Crafts architects drew on many diverse sources to design and decorate their new buildings. These included vernacular and folk structures such as barns, outbuildings and cottages, as well as native crafts such as tile making and overshot weaving. These principles carried a general nostalgia for a simpler time. Voysey saw the home as an art object. His buildings had soft warm tones, some with velvety thatched roofs. He and Baillie Scott designed their structures to incorporate many natural materials such as brick and stone as well as colored stucco. These materials integrated the house into the landscape. These men thought houses should be bright, light, cheerful, and easily cleaned. They should have comfort, simplicity, warmth, and an economy of upkeep. Homes should reveal their methods of construction and not be hidden under bric-a-brac and extensive ornamentation (fig. 5). These points became the basic tenets of the American Arts & Crafts and Bungalow movements of the early twentieth century. Voysey wrote a series of articles for the popular American magazine *Ladies' Home Journal* in 1901–2 about reforming architecture in the United States based on the English Arts & Crafts model. These new houses, he wrote, should provide a retreat

Fig. 5. Falcon Cliff House by M. H. Baillie Scott, a famous English Arts & Crafts architect. This 1897 building illustrates the use of natural materials and a simple exterior devoid of excessive Victorian decoration. (Photo by Patricia Tutt.)

Fig. 6. An "English Bungalow"
by Leonard Martin. This simple
vernacular-styled house featured stuccoed walls and a
thatched roof, both in keeping
with the Arts & Crafts
philosophy of unpretentious,
natural buildings. (Image from
Book of Bungalows, London.)

from the impersonal urban world and evoke Pugin's preindustrial countryside cottages. Voysey recommended homes with easy-care exterior surfaces as well as natural exposed beams and roof rafters. He stated that simple vernacular buildings like the bungalow were morally superior to the highly ornamented Queen Anne Victorian style (fig. 6). In his book *Arts and Crafts Architecture*, Peter Davey comments, "Voysey's works . . . were never symmetrical, for he was a firm believer in Ruskinian changefulness and praised Gothic Architecture because outside appearances are evolved from internal fundamental conditions; staircase and windows come where most convenient for use."

With America beginning to feel the full thrust of its own industrial revolution in the 1890s, the ideals and products of the British Arts & Crafts movement found fertile ground on this side of the Atlantic.

AMERICAN ARTS & CRAFTS

"It is gratifying to realize that the age of bizarre architecture is surely passing;

that we are being gradually educated into an appreciation of plain, simple

and dignified houses."

CHARLES ALMA BYERS, THE CRAFTSMAN, OCTOBER 1912

As the United States entered the last few years of the nineteenth century, a myriad of cultural changes were commencing that would redefine the nation for decades to come. As America became further industrialized, increasing numbers of individuals moved from the farm to the cities where jobs were plentiful and wages were on the rise. This migration created a population shift, with the South and West showing rapid expansion. When the demographics of the nation changed, so did its needs for housing. The typical large rural family with the sprawling gingerbread-covered farmhouse was no longer the norm for American domestic life. Singles and couples who worked as factory labor or in white-collar occupations chose to inhabit small, more efficient homes on narrow city lots or in the new suburban areas encircling major cities. The American Dream of owning a home became a reality at this point in our history.

The same industrialization that gave rise to the popularity of the motorcar and the bungalow also triggered a disquieting mood among American intellectuals, similar to the one experienced in Britain in the second half of the nineteenth century. Those who moved from the farm to the city had their schedules regimented by the time clock, not the seasons. Their labors, previously accomplished with their own hands, were replaced in many cases by repetitive, mindless work on a controlling machine. As factories began to sprout across America, the words of Pugin and Ruskin and other Arts & Crafts ideas from England began to have meaning in the New World. America's progressive political ideas began to mirror those of the Socialist Party in Britain. Discussions of nostalgia for the simpler life began to appear in the popular literature of the day, just as they had in England. However, as with most imported philosophies, Americans tended to fracture the British ideals and bend them to their own specific needs.

The Arts & Crafts era began in the United States in the late nineteenth century. Inspiration was drawn from the British model, but was characterized by its tendencies to adhere less strictly to English principles, and was to be more widely accepted by the public at large. Beginning with the 1876 Centennial celebrations in Philadelphia, Americans awakened to a growing sense of nationalism. The defining of the nation was evident with the addition of new states and the crisscrossing of the continent by rail

"Our Bungalow of Dreams"
(words by Tommie Malie and Charlie Newman, music by Joe Verges, 1927)

There's a place that I see every
night in my dreams, dear,

When I'm there every care
of the day disappears,

Tho it's built of dreams
it's in all my schemes,

How I pray for the day
we'll be on our way,

When the day fades away,
I feel gay as can be, dear,

For I know soon I'll go
to that nest far from here,

Castles in the air never
could compare,

In this land we have planned
we stroll hand in hand.

Chorus:
A little love nest beside a stream, where red,
red roses grow, our bungalow of dreams,

Far from the city somehow it seems,
we're sitting pretty in our bungalow of dreams.

Fig. 7. By 1917, the idea of owning your own home was considered a part of the American Dream. Montgomery Ward saw the trend and incorporated it into its advertising for Wardway Homes. For many Americans, the dream home was a bungalow.

lines. Military success in the Spanish American War thrust the U.S. onto the world scene, while massive immigration filled the country with a new diverse population. These rapid cultural changes resulted in Americans beginning to search for the nation's cultural and architectural roots. In the 1800s our nation experienced a progression of architectural styles that reflected mainly European designs. None of these home types appeared particularly suited to the new modern America of the 1890s. The Arts & Crafts philosophy, which promoted the use of vernacular, historical, or local architectural motifs and building materials, encouraged native architects to develop specific regional styles of architecture that more closely reflected the new urban America.

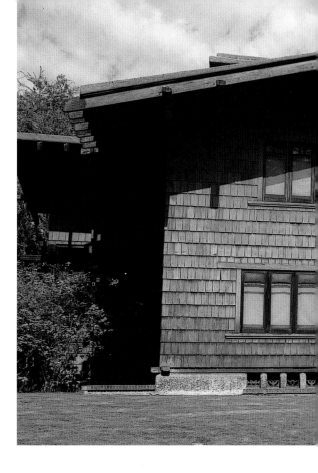

ARCHITECTURAL PHILOSOPHY OF THE AMERICAN ARTS & CRAFTS MOVEMENT

The American architects who followed the ideals of the Arts & Crafts Movement strove to develop an "organic" style of building, one that more closely reflected the landscape and the fabric from which the house was constructed. The use of indigenous building materials such as stone, brick, and stucco made the building seem more genuine. Because of the increasing pace of urban life, homes needed to be simple to maintain and designed in what the writers of the period labeled "common sense" style. This design theory called for the removal of the ornamentation found on earlier Queen Anne Victorian buildings. Arts & Crafts home designers pleaded for a contemporary architecture more fitted to the new suburban working-class lifestyle. Bertram Goodhue, an architect from Boston, wrote about the return to greater simplicity in home design. Others, like Louis Sullivan of Chicago, wanted buildings to be more natural. Frank Lloyd Wright designed his homes to be open to the landscape with simple exterior decoration. Many architects attempted to develop a truly American type of home unique to its geographical location. Periodical writers of the day talked about a "special

Fig. 8. Greene & Greene's Gamble House in Pasadena is considered to be a work of art by many. Its graceful lines and soft finishes are hallmarks of the Arts & Crafts philosophy.

domestic architecture" that suited the living conditions of the new American family. The touchstone word in these articles was "simple"—a house that could be inhabited without servants and expensive exterior maintenance. Some writers took the matter farther and appealed for a home that carried a rustic, almost barbaric character on the exterior. Escape to nature and rusticity also became a common theme. The modern home was expected to provide shelter and a retreat from the harsh urban world. Gone were Victorian gingerbread and ornate shingle patterns. Decorative brackets, if used at all, became simpler and columns on porches shorter and often simply square. All details were scaled down in size, shape, and level of embellishment.

Individualism was the hallmark of architectural style during this period. Designers worked to create a uniquely American style in the Arts & Crafts mode. The works of the Greene brothers, as summarized by Englishman C. R. Ashbee in 1909 after he visited them, echo sentiments concerning Arts & Crafts architecture as a whole. Ashbee called their southern California homes "tender, subtle, self-effacing and natural" (fig. 8).

Most Arts & Crafts houses, compared to their Victorian predecessors, were unpretentious. While British architects decried the use of machinery, many American designers chose to embrace it. While handwork was of the essence to the Greenes, they did use metal screws to hold beams in place. Frank Lloyd Wright used concrete and iron beams in his homes, and was outwardly in favor of employing machinery to create building parts. In America, simplicity could be achieved through the harmonious use of Arts & Crafts design philosophy and modern technology.

ARCHITECTS AND INFLUENTIAL HOME DESIGNERS OF THE ARTS & CRAFTS PERIOD

America produced many prestigious architects during the Arts & Crafts era. These designers set the tone for a building style that reflected the diverse regional interests of the nation. They also, in various ways, drew on the ideals of Morris, Ruskin, and other English spokesmen to enhance their designs. As a group, they created the homes that filled the American suburbs. While they did not literally design them, they influenced the scores of bungalows and Craftsman homes that were offered for sale in popular magazines, brochures, and catalogs right up until World War II.

Each architect influenced American home design in his or her own unique way. The Greene brothers in California took the fabrication and construction of the bungalow to an art form with graceful beams and rustic shingle and stonework. Their use of natural materials and soft natural colors helped create a prototype for the millions of bungalows that followed. Boston's leading architects Ralph Adam Cram and Bertram Goodhue assisted in the foundation of the Society of the Arts & Crafts in Boston in 1897. It was modeled on the Arts & Crafts Exhibition Society of London. The goal of these groups was to bring like-minded individuals together and to disseminate craft ideals through exhibitions, lectures, and discussions. Harvard fine arts professor Charles

Eliot Norton, a close friend of John Ruskin, was also a member. Norton helped the society offer classes and events that brought architects, craftsmen, and the public together on a personal, social level. The society also published a journal entitled *Handicraft* that featured essays from Morris, Ruskin, and other British notables. Detroit founded its society in 1906 and boasted such famous members as architects Albert Kahn and H. J. Maxwell Grylls, as well as Mary Chase Stratton, who founded Pewabic Pottery. This group carried on lively relationships that encouraged craftsmen from various fields to participate in the design and decoration of many of the area's grandest buildings.

Frank Lloyd Wright was a founding member of the Chicago Society of Arts & Crafts. His greatest fame came in the designs he developed for extremely simple Prairie-style homes. While lacking any historical association, they drew inspiration from the long, flat, horizontal midwestern landscape. Wright's homes conformed to nearly all the Arts & Crafts ideals. They employed native materials, open floor plans, and were, for the most part, without exterior ornamentation, yet were considered to be unique and of extreme beauty.

Although not an architect, Gustav Stickley had a large impact on house architecture in the first two decades of the twentieth century. Wisconsin-born and trained as a stonemason, Stickley preferred to work in wood. This choice led him to embrace the knowledge and ideals of the English Arts & Crafts proponents who favored handcrafting decorative items. Stickley visited England in 1898 and soon after founded *The Craftsman,* the magazine that became the standard bearer for the Arts & Crafts movement in America throughout its publishing history (1901–16). The magazine is highly prized today by collectors for its content and its handmade look. The first issue of *The Craftsman* was devoted to the works and philosophies of William Morris, while the second issue was devoted to those of John Ruskin. Stickley's fame was to come largely from two major sources—his Mission-style furniture and his home designs. Working with architect Harvey Ellis, Stickley published illustrations and building plans for new, modern house designs that today we would label as Craftsman homes. Ellis's designs appeared only briefly during the short period before his death, in 1903 and 1904, but

Stickley continued to publish house plans throughout the life of the magazine. So popular were they that two books were printed in 1909 and 1912. Titled *Craftsman Homes* and *More Craftsman Homes,* the publications offered a wide range of house types from simple cottages to Arts & Crafts–style bungalows and large Craftsman-style dwellings. These home plans followed the prevailing Arts & Crafts architectural philosophy of simple lines, non-ornate surfaces, and practical floor plans. They also suggested the use of some modern building materials like concrete and stucco. Stickley was also influential in bringing the works of noted British and American architects to his readers' attention by including articles on the homes of the Greenes, Wright, Ashbee, and others (figs. 9, 10).

Fig. 9. Gustav Stickley's *Craftsman* magazine published many innovative house plans during its operation from 1901 to 1916. This bungalow, originally published in *The Craftsman*, has an abundance of windows yet a simple overall feel as compared to its Victorian counterparts.

Fig. 10. Besides simple bungalows, Stickley also provided plans for large Craftsman-style homes. This model from 1916 has a low-maintenance stucco siding and a distinct lack of exterior ornamentation.

Another major source of house-plan information at the turn of the century was the mass-circulation magazine *Ladies' Home Journal.* In 1889 publisher Cyrus Curtis hired Edward Bok as editor. Bok quickly set about upgrading the publication and soon made it the first periodical to reach one million in circulation. The *Journal* began offering house plans in 1895, and Bok's goal was to improve small-house architecture in America

Fig. 11. Another popular source for Arts & Crafts– period home plans and ideas was *Ladies' Home Journal.* So admired were their designs that a book of their most popular plans was printed. This side-gabled bungalow is typical of the homes of the World War I period.

Fig. 12. A more rustic and oriental version of the bungalow is shown in *Ladies' Home Journal* in 1916. The entire house is very structural, with every piece of wood distinctly illustrated in the picture. This type of building tended to be colored in natural brown with little highlighting of the trim.

by having reputable, professional architects design the homes he featured. Residences by William Lightfoot Price, Walter Keith, and Frank Lloyd Wright appeared on its pages. *Ladies' Home Journal* published 169 plans by eighty-two architects over a twenty-five-year period. At first many were traditional Colonial Revival style but, beginning around 1900, the focus shifted to the Craftsman and Bungalow styles that featured sleeping porches, central heating, and multiple bathrooms. The magazine even published a book entitled *Journal Bungalows,* featuring the most modern plans by certified architects (figs. 11, 12). As a result of his work at *Ladies' Home Journal,* Edward Bok was credited by noted architect Stanford White as having "more completely influenced American domestic architecture for the better than any man in his generation."

Besides the mass-circulation magazines, there were specific niche publications for small houses and bungalows. *Keith's Beautiful Homes,* published in Minneapolis, was a monthly magazine that carried a variety of articles about bungalow design, landscaping, and decorating. It offered home plans and even bungalow plan books for sale. The most famous of the niche journals was *Bungalow Magazine,* published in Seattle and costing twenty-five cents per issue (fig. 13). Begun in 1912, its first-year circulation reached nearly thirty thousand. Every issue carried an article called "Featured Bungalow" that included mini-blueprints and specifications for new homes. In the May 1914 issue, the author of an article entitled "Study in Gray" suggested, "Color is the complexion of the building," and further noted that using the wrong color gives the house a sick effect. As a positive example, he recommended a soft gray body with white trim. Other articles covered landscaping, Swiss-style bungalows, interior design, and colors. Advertisements at the rear of the publication illustrated the large number of house design sources in the pre–World War I period with such companies as Egyptian Stucco Bungalows of Los Angeles, Miller's Bungalow Plans of Omaha, and Jens C. Peterson, a Detroit architect offering plan books (fig. 14).

Beyond acquiring house plans and building locally through a contractor, new homebuyers had an additional option. Mass-market national retailers such as Sears, Roebuck and Co. and Montgomery Ward offered homes for sale in kit form. The town

Fig. 13. *Bungalow Magazine* began publishing in 1912 and catered exclusively to the modest- and small-homes market.

of Bay City, Michigan, boasted three companies that sold Bungalow and Craftsman kit homes nationwide in the first four decades of the twentieth century—Aladdin, Sterling, and Lewis & Liberty. The sheer volume in terms of variety of house types and styles offered by these companies is staggering, with hundreds of models for sale via annually published catalogs. Prospective purchasers could view homes in color lithographs, and some companies even suggested specific color schemes for their various models. Aladdin Homes pictured a full-color, two-page spread of paint choices in many of its catalogs (fig. 15). Sears, Roebuck and Co. homebuyers received enough paint with each kit house to provide for two coats. These catalogs that circulated in the hundreds of thousands are useful tools to ascertain the popular home styles and colors of the Arts & Crafts period.

The development in America of a new mass-housing market with new architectural styles was made possible by a number of factors, all converging at the same time. The rapid rise of industrial

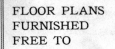

and white-collar jobs in urban areas brought massive numbers of workers into areas of the nation that lacked adequate housing. The developing transportation system of streetcars, interurban trolleys, and automobiles allowed workers the possibility of living farther away from their places of employment than ever before. Advances in wood harvesting and distribution via a nationwide rail system allowed inexpensive building materials to reach nearly every corner of the country. The standardization of building materials, such as 2 x 4 lumber and wire nails, allowed for a revolution in housing by lowering costs and raising quality. These factors brought less expensive, more practical homes within the reach of hundreds of thousands of families at the turn of the century. The ability of mass-circulation magazines to reach nearly every family in the nation allowed for the dissemination of new ideas about home design and style. Advertising allowed companies in Chicago and Bay City, Michigan, to sell homes by mail and ship them in kits to anywhere a rail line would take the pieces. These technological factors, combined with the influences of the British Arts & Crafts philosophy, produced the largest number of housing starts in the nation's history up to that point.

Fig 14 (above). Potential homebuyers had a vast array of choices in the early years of the twentieth century. This back inside cover of *Bungalow Magazine* from 1912 illustrates just a few of the house-plans books available.

Fig. 15 (right). Aladdin Readi-Cut Homes in 1916 provided color options for their kit houses.

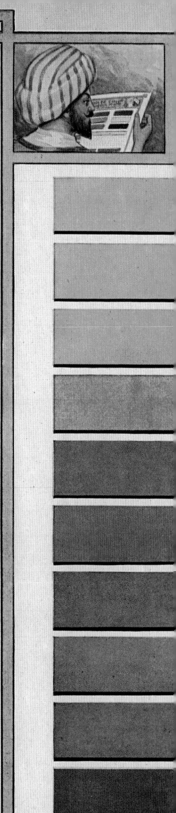

Aladdin Pa

Readi Colored Lead in Paste Form is ground in pure raw li̖ seed oil, to the consistency of white lead. There is no more durable ̖cal and practical combination of paint pigments in paste form. Aladdin Readi Colored Lead is guaranteed to give perfect satisfaction.

CREAM
For Trim Use
Flesh Tint
Centennial Brown
White

FAWN
For Trim Use
Flesh Tint
Dark Terra Cotta
Centennial Brown

WILLOW GREEN
For Trim Use
Med. Quaker Drab
Olive Drab
Golden Olive

GOLDEN OLIVE
For Trim Use
Olive Drab
Cream

CANARY
For Trim Use
Flesh Tint
Buff
Centennial Brown

CENTENNIAL BROWN
For Trim Use
Buff
Dark Terra Cotta
Cream

OLIVE DRAB
For Trim Use
Silver Gray
French Gray
Lemont Stone

WHITE

FLESH TINT
For Trim Use
French Gray
Buff
Fawn

DARK TERRA COTTA
For Trim Use
Fawn
Red
Cream

WARM DRAB
For Trim Use
French Gray
Lead Color
Leather Brown
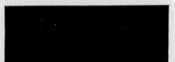

BLACK

RENCH GRAY
For Trim Use
White
Lavender
Silver Gray

RED
For Trim Use
White
French Gray
Golden Olive

Johnson's Wood Dyes for Aladdin Homes

Johnson's Wood Dye is made in various standard shades. We have adopted the six shades shown below on Oregon Fir, this being the wood furnished by us for all Aladdin houses. These shades are especially adapted for coloring Oregon Fir. Johnson's Wood Dye is a Dye in every sense of the word. It penetrates so deeply that the natural color is not disclosed if the wood becomes scratched or marred. It brings out the beauty of the grain, and should not be confused with Varnish Stains which remain on the surface, giving a painty, cheap looking effect which shows every scratch and mar.

The finish of the interior woodwork in Aladdin houses has been given serious and careful attention, and after investigating the best known brands of Wood Dye, Stain and other finishes, we have decided to supply only the JOHNSON'S WOOD DYE with each of our houses, knowing that they are entirely different and superior to any other article now on the market.

JOHNSON'S WOOD DYE does not contain any finish whatever—like most first class products, it answers one purpose only—it dyes the wood—a finish must be applied over it.

ILWAUKEE BRICK
For Trim Use
Lemont Stone
Med. Quaker Drab
Leather Brown

SEAL BROWN
For Trim Use
White
Cream
Buff

BUFF
For Trim Use
Cream
Flesh Tint
Leather Brown

LEATHER BROWN
For Trim Use
Cream
Centennial Brown
White

PEARL GRAY
For Trim Use
White
French Gray
Lead Color

SILVER GRAY
For Trim Use
Lemont Stone
Lead Color
French Gray

No. 123 DARK OAK

No. 131 WALNUT

EMONT STONE
For Trim Use
Lead Color
Olive Drab
Med. Quaker Drab

MED. QUAKER DRAB
For Trim Use
Milwaukee Brick
Warm Drab
Leather Brown

No. 128 LIGHT MAHOGANY & CHERRY

No. 129 DARK MAHOGANY

LAVENDER
For Trim Use
Silver Gray
Warm Drab
French Gray

PEA GREEN
For Trim Use
Milwaukee Brick
Med. Quaker Drab
Willow Green

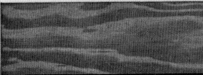

No. 126 LIGHT OAK

No. 125 MISSION OAK

LEAD COLOR
For Trim Use
Lavender
Olive Drab
Pearl Gray

OLIVE
For Trim Use
White
Silver Gray
Golden Olive

Home Styles
& Exterior Colors

"We suggest that instead of the siding you have the entire surface shingled.

The roof may be stained a soft forest green and the side walls a light brown or

tan hue without any tint of yellow. This will harmonize nicely with the brick

of your column supports and chimneys. The green of the roof can be repeated,

with good effect, in the window frames, and we advise that the sash be painted

white so as to give a strongly defined line and accent to the windows. You will

find that these colors will receive a nice setting when

your trees and shrubbery get far enough advanced to

give some effective mass of color."

"Replies and Discussion," The Craftsman, June 1905

Four basic categories of Arts & Crafts houses are commonly found on the landscape today—the Bungalow, the Craftsman, the Foursquare, and the Postmodern Bungalow. This section describes the physical characteristics of each house style, provides a history of each type, and includes information about historical design sources and styles, including the colors traditionally used for the house's body, trim, and accents.

THE BUNGALOW

The bungalow is commonly defined as a single-story house, usually small with a wide front porch and a low-pitched sloping roof. However, many bungalows are one-and-a-half stories, and in the early decades of the twentieth century were called semi-bungalows. Today we combine them in the standard bungalow classification.

This versatile house type has been associated with the establishment of home ownership, which was considered a major component of the American Dream. The key to the bungalow's popularity was the philosophy that simplicity and craftsmanship could

Fig. 17. A single-story bungalow. The steep roof pitch limits the use of the second floor. The front-gabled windows are more for show than ventilation.

Fig. 16. An example of a semi-bungalow, or one-and-a-half-story model. The use of larger shed-roofed dormers opens up the top floor for bedrooms.

harmonize in an affordable house. These small, usually informal homes came in a wide range of sizes and styles. They were considered comfortable, picturesque, honest, and distinctively American. The bungalow was sensible, efficient, and came to symbolize "the good life" for many in the new century (figs. 16, 17).

History of the Bungalow

Scholars disagree about the origins of the bungalow. The most prevailing opinion is that this type of house was first developed in India and used widely as a traveler's hut during the period of British rule. The building type as well as the name derive from a Hindi word meaning "a house in the Bengali style." These common native dwellings featured wide eaves and large porches especially suited for that tropical climate. The building form was exported first to England and then to America in the latter part of the nineteenth century. Once in the United States, it was transformed into the economical Arts & Crafts house.

Another opinion suggests that the basic shape of the bungalow was already being built in post–Civil War Victorian America and was adapted by adding Craftsman features to it, a style popularized in the various magazines, plan books, and kit-house catalogs of the early twentieth century. This home type became popular when Americans began to desire a smaller, more economical type of dwelling that better reflected the modern working family's lifestyle. Bungalows began as vacation homes in the late 1880s, and then shifted to residences around 1900. Their greatest period of popularity was in the middle teens through the 1920s, with the most artistic era in the 1905 to 1915 period. This type of house continued to be built into the 1930s, but began to fade from public favor during the Great Depression. Colonial Revival–style homes that were reminiscent of a bygone age, such as the Cape Cod, began to replace bungalows.

Types or Classes of Bungalows

Because the bungalow is more a type of house than a style, it takes many forms and shapes. A house type refers more to a building's shape and massing than to its decorative features. The two major ways to classify bungalows are by roof form, which directly reflects the house's shape, and by decorative style features. Six general roof classifications are commonly employed to identify bungalows:

Front Gable (Fig. 18) Side Gable (Fig. 19)

Shed Roof (Fig. 20)

Double Front Gable (Fig. 21)

Double Cross Gable (airplane) (Fig. 22)

Pyramid/Hipped (Fig. 23)

This classification scheme allows us to distinguish the various categories of bungalows and to identify the wide variety of its plans or footprints. These roof types or massing shapes customarily have a "decorative style" overlay on them. Attached to the six roof classifications could be any of a number of decorative style detailings, including:

- Spanish
- English Tudor
- Colonial
- Arts & Crafts
- Swiss
- Prairie
- Rustic

These decorative styles were popular at various times during the Bungalow period from 1890 to the 1930s, not necessarily all at the same time.

Far and away the most popular decorative style was the Arts & Crafts bungalow, built in great numbers starting at the end of the first decade of the twentieth century. Its simple decorative features consisted of some or all of the following:

- Wide front porches
- Porches having half walls and short columns on piers
- Rustic stone and brickwork
- Projecting, exposed roof rafters
- Large knee-style brackets at the cornice
- Side bay windows (usually in the dining room)
- An abundance of windows (some in groups or bands)
- Pergolas
- Prominent chimney (stone or brick)
- Front-facing shed-roof dormers
- Sleeping porches
- Low-pitched roofs
- Wide overhanging eaves
- Mixtures of siding types (clapboard, wood shingles, stucco, and concrete)

On the Trail of the Home Design

Figure 24: Many methods were used to acquire bungalow plans in the early years of the twentieth century. This comic from the 1916 *American Carpenter & Builder* magazine suggests how *not* to do it.

Sources of Bungalow Designs

Prospective home builders in the early twentieth century could consult with a wide assortment of suppliers in order to secure their house plans. They could engage the services of an architect and have a bungalow designed specifically to their taste. While this method produced some of the most artistic types, it was not the most popular way to select one's house, as this method was costly and out of reach for most homebuyers. Some architects did sell bungalow plans (specifications and blueprints) to clients through a printed plans book. These inexpensive volumes were advertised in the back of popular magazines of the day such as *House Beautiful* or *Better Homes & Gardens.* Companies such as Standard Home Plans, National Plan Service, Curtis Companies, and Brown Blodgett printed collections of bungalow plans and offered those for sale via catalogs available at lumberyards and through the mail. Customers could pick from a wide selection of houses shown in these publications and order the complete blueprint plans directly from the company's home office. Some of the popular magazines of the period such as *Ladies' Home Journal* ran articles about the houses and sold plans books of their own. *Ladies' Home Journal* and Stickley's *Craftsman* magazine publicized a "Featured Home" in each issue.

Yet another method to secure not only the plans but also parts for a bungalow was through one of the kit-house companies. At least seven of these companies advertised nationally between 1910 and 1940, including Aladdin, Sterling Homes, and Lewis Homes, as well as the more famous Wardway Homes by Montgomery Ward and Sears, Roebuck and Co.'s Modern Homes. These companies would sell you the entire package, including lumber, siding, roof shingles, doors, and windows, right down to the nails and the paint.

Finally, there were several monthly periodical publications devoted to either new homes or bungalows exclusively. Such examples as *Keith's Magazine of Home Building* and *Bungalow Magazine* catered to the growing demand for housing in the early twentieth century. These sources produced thousands of bungalow plans and made them available to the general public in a simple format.

Bungalow Popularity

There is no doubt what the most popular housing type in America was in the first part of the twentieth century. While traditional house types such as the Georgian

Colonial remained fashionable, and even some Victorian designs continued to be built into the 1920s, the bungalow dominated the landscape from California to Florida and Michigan to Texas. A good illustration of this popularity can be seen in a review of the available bungalow plans offered for sale by six of the kit-house companies in 1916. These sellers offered 172 different bungalow plans that year. This number equaled 35 percent of all the house types offered for sale in 1916. Montgomery Ward in 1918 offered twenty-six different bungalow models out of a total of fifty in their Wardway kit-homes catalog. A look through any magazine or plans book of the early-twentieth-century era shows an abundance of bungalow styles and types. As early as 1904, the bungalow was being touted at the best type of house for the general public. *Keith's Magazine* offered these helpful hints: "It is much more difficult to make a large house cozy then a small one, and a house to be comfortable must be cozy." The compact, efficient nature of the bungalow made it the right choice for homeowners for many years. This widespread popularity was enduring, as bungalow neighborhoods and courts continued to be built well into the 1930s and up to the eve of World War II.

Bungalow Colors

In the first decade of the twentieth century, *Keith's Magazine* made it clear to homeowners that more than just the interior of one's house was important. "You own the exterior as well as the interior of your home and both will provide for you if you will give your architect the opportunity," an article in the magazine stated. The publisher believed that an architect, a person of training and taste, could arrange the house colors in a harmonious blend and that homeowners could benefit from this person's experience.

To characterize all bungalow colors broadly would be difficult. Fashionable colors and popular shades shifted throughout the 1890 to 1940 period. Different sources, plan books, paint-company brochures, and kit-house catalogs pictured bungalows in a variety of colors for a wide range of reasons. Companies like Sears, Roebuck and Co.

wanted their homes to be bright and cheerful to attract potential customers. Paint companies wanted to sell their product and therefore illustrated houses in multiple color schemes. Those factors need to be considered when viewing original source materials for color ideas. An extensive number of surface materials were in use on bungalow exteriors, and each surface contributed to the overall effect of the color scheme. The most popular exterior siding types were clapboards, both thin and wide, and/or shingles in a simple square or rectangular style (not necessarily the fancy Victorian types). Stucco on lath and concrete were likewise in wide use and both of these materials could either be painted or tinted during the mixing process to provide color.

BODY COLORS

Early bungalows tended to follow the strict doctrine of Arts & Crafts naturalistic colors. Earth tones such as browns and darker greens were favored. Around World War I, colors began to lighten, with yellows, sages, and tans beginning to be utilized. Figure 27 illustrates the use of yellow as the major body color. Two-toning became popular beginning around 1915, with the various siding styles being singled out for their

Fig. 27. In the early 1910s, body colors on bungalows began to lighten. This example from the Portland Cement Company illustrates a popular medium yellow.

Fig. 28. Two-toning, or dividing the house into two color zones, became popular around 1915. This effect, seen here in a dark top over light bottom, creates the illusion of a long low structure.

own specific color. Figure 28 shows the clear distinction that employing two contrasting colors on each level can achieve. This color placement allows the bungalow to maintain its horizontal orientation even though it is not a single-story design.

On one-and-a-half-story bungalows, the upper floors were usually set off by a trim board divider and a dissimilar type of siding in a different color. No solid rule is evident about which value went on the top. In some examples the darker color was on top and in others it was employed on the bottom siding. Combining siding types such as stucco, shingles, and clapboards was common. These various surface materials, united with brick and stonework, provided interesting multicolored bodies on many homes. There are a few examples in which a monochrome body color was employed. Homes that emulated the Prairie style of Frank Lloyd Wright were often constructed of concrete or surfaced with stucco; in some of these the concrete was left natural or tinted a light color such as gray or cream. Additional color was added to the trim and details. Figure 29 demonstrates a Prairie-style home with a concrete body accented with an olive roof and trim. This minimalist view of coloring the bungalow was in line with architect Wright's philosophy of a simple, low-maintenance exterior. Another example of a single body color is shown in figure 30. This cross-gable bungalow is painted in a dark green with

Fig. 29. The Prairie style, made popular by Frank Lloyd Wright, is shown here in a monochrome body color. Masonry-sided homes were often left natural or had tinted stucco or concrete for color.

Fig. 30. An example of a one-color body on a bungalow. Even with only one major color, the awnings, brickwork, two colors of trim, and natural concrete porch provide visual interest.

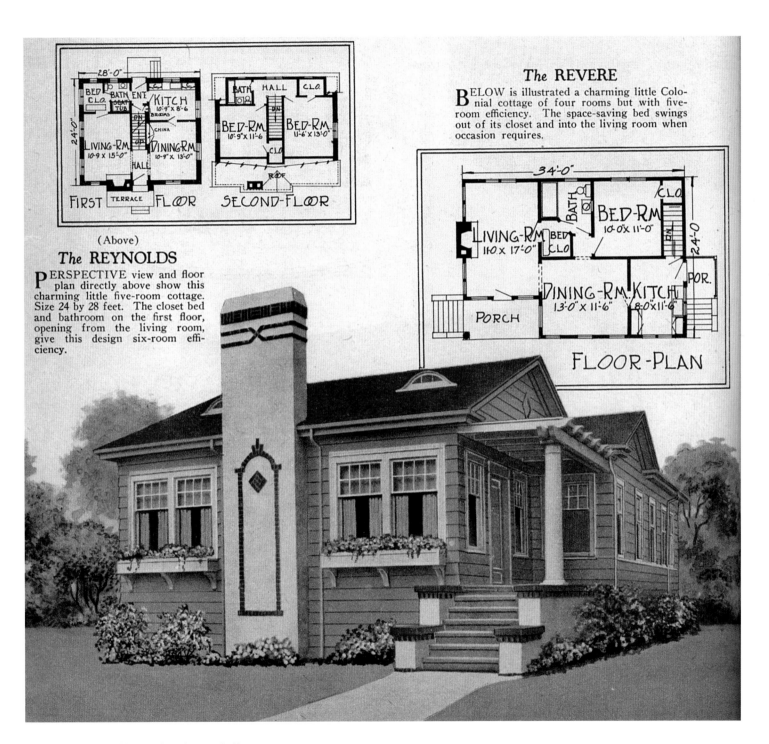

The REVERE

BELOW is illustrated a charming little Colonial cottage of four rooms but with five-room efficiency. The space-saving bed swings out of its closet and into the living room when occasion requires.

(Above)

The REYNOLDS

PERSPECTIVE view and floor plan directly above show this charming little five-room cottage. Size 24 by 28 feet. The closet bed and bathroom on the first floor, opening from the living room, give this design six-room efficiency.

Fig. 31. This 1926 plate from *American Builder* magazine is an example of the changing taste in Arts & Crafts color schemes. It features a light green body, off-white trim, and red accents.

no distinction between the body and the upper gables. This scheme has the effect of bringing the house down to the landscape and making it seem more a part of its surroundings. Additional color variety was achieved through the use of tinted stucco on the porch and brick on piers and wall caps.

In the late 1920s and into the 1930s, bungalow body colors continued to change. Colors such as medium green, salmon, and even cream came into favor. Figures 31 and 32 are good examples of this shift in taste. Figure 31 combines a red roof with a medium-green body, contrasting stucco, and brick chimney for a very lively façade. Figure 32 demonstrates the use of tinted stucco and large-dimension shingle siding with a roof that resembles wood shakes. The darker tones of the previous period were not entirely eliminated, but were combined with light colors in two-tone schemes. This mixing of colors in numerous combinations by period designers is reflective of the myriad of colorful looks available to homeowners.

Fig. 32. As bungalow designs changed, so did their exterior colors. This late-1920s home featured clipped gables, fancy shutters, an orange and cream body, and medium brown trim.

TRIM AND ACCENT COLORS

With the naturalistic colors of the earliest bungalows came trims of an equally natural character. These homes were colored without a great deal of contrast between the body and trim. Houses could have a different color on the trim, but it would most likely be a similar value as the body color. What was considered trim varied by source, but generally the corner boards, the eaves, and the boards around the windows and doors were treated differently than the body. The bungalow in figure 33 employs a shade of white on all the standard trim elements, making them easy to identify.

Fig. 33. This bungalow employs white on all the standard trim elements, making them easy to identify.

The window sash was usually painted in a different color than the window trim. The sash color seemed to have taken its cue from the prevailing Victorian preference for a dark tone. The most popular bungalow window-sash colors were dark red, dark green, dark brown, or black. The Marsden model, produced by Aladdin Homes around 1915, illustrates the use of black window sash with highly contrasting, light trim (fig. 34). Doors, including screen and storm doors, were made of wood, and, for the most part, stained in a medium to dark color. Some exterior doors were painted and their colors tended to be in harmony with the rest of the color scheme. The modern fashion of a bright red door was not considered acceptable in the early years of the twentieth century.

Fig. 34. This Marsden model from Aladdin Homes employs white on all the standard trim elements and black for the window sash, contrasting against a reddish brown body.

Bungalows of the late 1910s were often painted with more contrast—light bodies and darker trim colors. Figure 35 illustrates that look with a vellum body, dark-green heavy trim work topped by a red roof, and wonderful redbrick porches. This sandwich effect, a red top and bottom with green and vellum middle, is striking. Looking at bungalow pictures from the 1920s, one discerns a trend toward lighter trims with the introduction of vellum, white, and off-white shades. Sears, Roebuck and Co.'s popular Elsmore model, fig. 36, one of the few models illustrated in color in their *Modern Homes* catalog, employed a dark green body reminiscent of the earlier era, but now featured off-white trim and gray stucco to attract buyers. Some homes of this period exhibited accent colors on brackets and roof rafters that were different than the regular trim color. In some cases these were darker, and in some cases, like figure 33, they were

Fig. 35. This handsome bungalow is colored in a scheme that was popular around 1910. It is highly contrasting with a very light body and dark trim. Additional color is provided in the red roof and brick.

Fig. 36. Sears, Roebuck and Co.'s popular Elsmore model featured a dark green body, reminiscent of early bungalows, but was adorned with an off-white trim in the 1920s style.

lighter. Items such as pergolas were treated in a similar fashion, with some examples painted in the light family of colors and some shown in the darker tones. Figure 35 illustrates the side pergola, a semi-covered porch, being colored in dark green to match the rest of the trim, while the home in figure 31 on page 53 has it in white. Generally the pergola was colored to match the house trim, but that was not always the case.

Porches were considered extended living spaces, just as they had been in the previous Victorian period. Bungalow porches came in a wide variety of shapes and sizes. Some carried simple railings between porch columns, some no railings at all, while others had solid knee-high walls. Many of the period publications illustrated these porches in only one color, but research has proven that they were sometimes painted in several colors. The fussy coloring of each porch spindle and column in multiple colors, so fancied in the Victorian period, was not common in the bungalow, whose columns were usually shorter, placed on piers of brick or stone, and often painted in off-white or vellum. Any railing areas might be colored in a monochrome fashion with rails and spindles in the same color. Examples do exist that show the rails being a darker color than the spindles. Porch floors were usually painted a dark color such as red, gray, or green. Ceilings, when painted, were done in soft tones to reflect the light, and some even had electric fixtures installed to provide evening illumination. Many bungalow porch ceilings were stained wood with a glossy varnish. The porch acted as an additional room, so it often contained oriental rugs, tables, and chairs, in season. Awnings such as those shown in figures 30 (p. 52) and 32 (p. 54) added color to the overall plan as well as providing shade. Most awnings were striped.

ROOFING MATERIALS AND COLORS

Bungalow designers considered the roof an integral part of the overall look and feel of the house. As opposed to the elaborately gabled and sometimes multicolored Victorian roof, bungalows had simpler roof designs and colors. Early bungalows were often sheathed in wood shingles to provide a naturalistic covering to the house. When aged, they turned a variety of shades of gray to brown, depending on the type of wood employed. Because of the wide range of roofing materials available during this era, there is no single correct "bungalow roof." Metal roofs and composition shingles, in addition to wood, were also in common use. A review of period sources shows a tendency to have roofs in "colors" in the late teens and into the twenties and thirties. Red and green, as well as multi-mix combinations of browns and grays, seemed to be favorite choices (figs. 25, 26).

Fig. 25. Bungalow-era roofs were colorful. The cover of this Sears, Roebuck and Co. roofing catalog shows both a red and a green example.

Fig. 26. This Craftsman home was illustrated in a roofing brochure to demonstrate its use of mixed-color shingles. As a cap to a very plain wall surface, it provides an exciting, colorful alternative.

ROOFING

SEARS, ROEBUCK AND CO.
CHICAGO.

THE CRAFTSMAN HOME

The Craftsman home is defined as a two-story home with Arts & Crafts detailing and/or one of the types shown in Stickley's *Craftsman* magazine. Numerous Craftsman homes have masonry exteriors of stucco, cement, and brick combinations, with low-pitched roofs and grouped windows. Many also have attached semi-covered porches called pergolas. Some 1920s versions had attached and enclosed sun porches. Overhanging eaves were supported by large simple brackets and/or false beaming and, like the bungalow, were built with exposed roof-rafter ends. Because of their size, these homes were often constructed on larger suburban lots. While Bungalows were normally limited to three or fewer bedrooms, the Craftsman-style homes offered more square footage and usually four or more bedrooms. In many areas it replaced the Colonial as the large house of choice during that period.

Fig. 37. An example of a Craftsman-style home. The clean uncluttered exterior was a dramatic shift away from the ornate Victorian and Colonial Revival homes of the nineteenth century.

Fig. 38. This early Craftsman design features bands of windows, shingle siding, and exposed roof-rafter ends. It is reminiscent of the Greene brothers' work in California.

In the first two decades of the twentieth century, the term "Craftsman home" generally referred to only those plans offered in Stickley's *Craftsman* from 1901 to 1916. Stickley introduced less ornate, more modern homes to the general public through illustrations in his monthly magazine and in the books he published. Many of the house plans shown in Stickley's publications were single- and one-and-a-half-story bungalows, but a respectable number of them were two-story homes. Other sources like magazines, plans books, and architectural publications also offered two-story plans during this period and called them by a variety of names, such as Craft-modern and Arts & Crafts. Over time the term *Craftsman* was adopted by architectural historians to help better define the housing types of the early twentieth century. At the turn of the twenty-first century, any larger two-story homes with Arts & Crafts exterior features built in the period between 1900 and 1940 are now labeled as Craftsman.

Types of Craftsman Homes

Unlike bungalows, the Craftsman house did not come in as many subclasses. There were only two basic formats—a front-facing-gable type and a side-gable or roof-ridge-to-street style. Some variations did exist, such as the **L** or **T** footprint plans, and those that employed roof gables either butted into the roof ridge or as cross gables. Because of the two-story design, multiple siding types were popular in combinations of stucco, shingles, clapboard, and cement. Surprisingly, many Craftsman homes have smaller front porches than did their bungalow counterparts. This type of house has many of the same detail features as the bungalow:

- Projecting, exposed roof rafters
- Large knee-style brackets at the cornice
- Sleeping porches
- Horizontal lines

Fig. 39. This Craftsman home is an example of the front-facing gable type. Its wide simple plan allows for a dramatic front porch and clipped gables.

- Mixtures of siding types
- Less prominent front porches
- Grouped or band of windows
- Prominent chimneys
- Pergolas
- Rustic stone and brickwork
- Side bay windows

Sources of Craftsman Designs and Popularity

The same magazines, plans books, and kit-house catalogs that offered bungalows also sold Craftsman plans. Sears, Roebuck and Co., Aladdin, and *Ladies' Home Journal* customers could choose from an impressive variety of alternatives. Books like Gustav Stickley's *Craftsman Homes* and *More Craftsman Homes* also provided consumers with a variety of house plans illustrating Craftsman-style homes. This house type dropped from public favor as the twenties drew to a close and was replaced by designs more Colonial and English in influence.

Craftsman Colors

Because these homes were generally larger than their bungalow counterparts, they could by and large accommodate more complex color schemes, but that was not necessarily the case. Research from historic sources suggests three basic types of Craftsman color schemes.

The first retained the stucco and concrete in its natural color and just added a trim and perhaps an accent color. Figure 40, from the Radford Company of Chicago, is a prime example. While enlivened with striped awnings, the home is otherwise quite stark in appearance. Hard surfaces could be heavily colored as well, and figure 41 shows a 1912 Sherwin-Williams example in dark green with highly contrasting trim in two light shades. The addition of a darker-green roof aids in making the house look long and low.

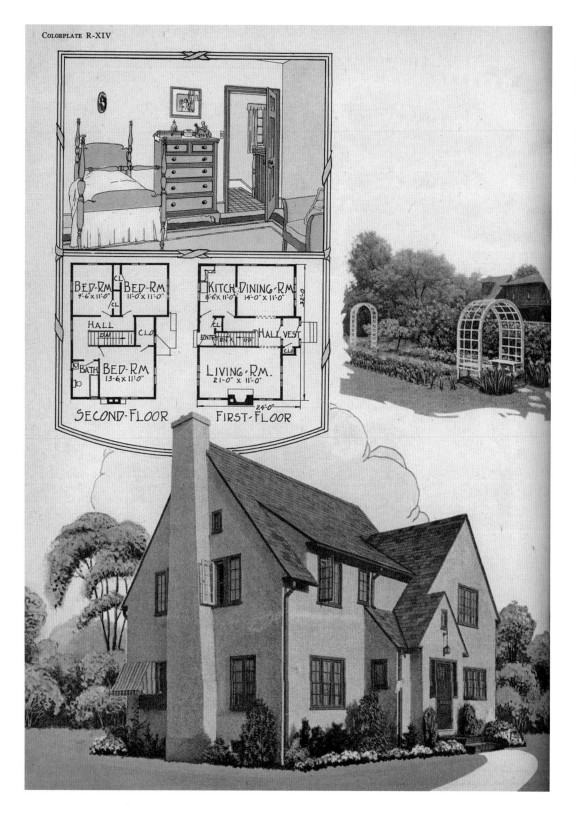

Fig. 40. One of the three major types of Craftsman color schemes, this design leaves the stucco surface in its natural gray color while highlighting the windows and building edges in green.

Fig. 41. This 1912
masonry-sided Craftsman with
a dark green body and
off-white trim is pictured in a
Sherwin-Williams paint
brochure. The use of black for
the window sash adds even
more interest.

The second, and most popular, color scheme for this style was two-tone coloration. Craftsman houses were often divided visually between floors, and the two-tone scheme usually contrasted a dark story against a light story. Figure 42 shows a reduced-size first floor colored in terra-cotta under a larger, light yellow top section. Figure 43, a design from about 1920, illustrates just the opposite effect with a white first story under a dark green top story. A third example of two-tone coloration displays a yellowish-orange top over a dark brown bottom. One additional way to employ two-tone colors is shown in figure 44, where the second color is used only in the top gable and porch gable of the house. The body is one color, a medium yellow, and the muddy brown is used to accentuate the trim and cap the building. A review of period color sources turns up a wide range of color combinations for the two-tone house.

The third major color scheme for Craftsman homes was a more conservative variation on the two-tone concept. Closely matched colors were painted on both sections of the house body. Figure 45, from the Aladdin Company, shows two shades of brown on its Georgia No. 2 model from 1916. A Portland Cement Company brochure from about 1915 shows a large Craftsman-style house in two shades of gray. This scheme works because the red roof and light foundation offsets the somber gray tones of the body. However, a gray or black roof would result in too monochromatic a color scheme.

Fig. 42. The two-tone Craftsman color scheme was very popular. This example from 1912 uses a light-over-dark combination with an off-white trim. Note that the second-floor balcony is in yellow, not the off-white trim color.

Fig. 43. A dark top/light bottom color scheme can have a stunning effect. This model home from 1920 employs highly contrasting dark green and off-white. The green is also painted at the foundation level and on the porch columns. Note the terra-cotta color under the eaves area.

Fig. 45. This Aladdin kit house from 1916 illustrates a conservative two-tone color scheme with slight variations of brown on each floor.

Fig. 44. Colored in the Arts & Crafts autumn palette of yellow-orange and brown, this home employs the two-tone style in a different manner, with only the gables and bay in the darker color.

TRIM AND ACCENT COLORS

As in all homes of the period, the Craftsman style was painted with contrasting colors on its trim pieces. Off-whites, creams, vellums, and lighter colors were used when the body colors were dark, and green or brown when the body was light. The darker trim versions were typically executed in the pre–World War I era and the lighter versions afterwards. Occasionally a very dark trim was employed with a dark body color such as in figure 46 from 1912, which has a red-brown trim against a green upper body. The use of a shortened first floor in yellow allows the trim color to complement both body colors equally. Window sash was generally dark-colored, with black, dark green, and brown being the most popular options. In the late teens and into the twenties, whites and off-whites began to appear on the sash. Because of the large size of most Craftsman houses and the simplicity in ornamentation, featuring small details was disadvantageous, as they would be lost in the sheer volume of the structure. Even so, some accent coloring was attempted.

Figure 43 from around 1920 illustrates two trends. This green-and-white house has the under-eaves area colored in terra-cotta and the porch columns in dark green. Figure 42 has shutters on the upper-story windows colored in medium olive to contrast with the off-white trim and yellow stucco. The house in figure 46 has front steps in a contrasting shade of red-brown, which sets them off sharply against the yellow porch sides. Craftsman steps were colored in a variety of methods to attract attention to the main entryway, which was substantially smaller and less ornate than the previous highly decorative Queen Anne Victorian homes of the 1880s.

Fig. 46. An example of a dark body/dark trim paint scheme from about 1912. The use of dark trim colors was common in the pre–World War I era.

Fig. 47. This two-tone gray-body Craftsman home employs a red roof with highlighted seams in white to enliven an otherwise somber color scheme. Without the red roof, the home would look rather bland.

ROOFING MATERIALS AND COLORS

Craftsman roofs ranged from primarily simple gables to a few complex multi-hipped affairs, and most were low pitched. Roofs were often in darker colors to assist in visually lowering the house while trying to keep it in balance. In the age before the skyscraper, height was an important issue in home design. During this time, when major buildings were much shorter than they are today, the aspiration of a good plan was to have the house be "in scale" with its neighbors. Dark browns, reds, greens, and grays were all used to achieve that principle. Some examples, notably figure 47, illustrate a trend to highlight the seams of the roof hip with a contrasting color, in this case off-white to red. Composition shingles were common, as were wood shakes, slates, and tiles.

FOURSQUARE OR BOX HOUSE

This style's hallmarks include a two-story design, nearly square or rectangular in shape, that is longer than wide, not overly ornate, and having a generally low-pitched hip roof with dormers. Designers of the era described it as the perfect city house—practical, sturdy, and economical, with an ample porch. Its box-like design made every square inch of the plan usable.

History of the Foursquare

Fig. 48. Sterling Homes of Bay City, Michigan, produced some excellent examples of the Foursquare, or Box House. This type of house was known as practical, economical, and sturdy.

Known by a variety of names such as Edwardian, American Basic, Box House, and Corn-belt Cube, the Foursquare (its contemporary name) started appearing widely around the turn of the century. In the 1880s and 1890s, some Victorian house designs included a number of the same features as the Foursquare, such as the small shed-style roof dormer and the relatively flat, squarish façade with a trim-board divider between the floors. Historians believe that this type of house is a descendant of the Federal-style townhouse of the 1790s and the Civil War–era, Italianate Cube–style house with its ornate eaves brackets and arched windows. The twentieth-century Arts & Crafts version of the square house was ideally suited to urban environments and included the ability to squeeze three or four bedrooms into a really narrow plan. This was ideal for homes that had to be built on the thin urban lots that abutted streetcar and interurban lines.

The Foursquare shared the bungalow's virtues of practicality and simplicity, and even carried those ideals a bit further as Foursquare homes tended to be less ornate than their bungalow counterparts. Roofs, for example, were not as complex, and most were hipped or pyramid in shape. A small dormer might be built on any or all of its four sides. Roof eaves extended out over the walls just as in the bungalow, with exposed rafter ends and perhaps even simple knee-style brackets. The front porch usually ran across the entire width of the front façade, providing a convenient outdoor space and, if enclosed, a year-round sunroom. Other porches were built with columns on brick and stone piers, similar to those of the bungalow. Some porches had full-height square or round columns, making them look slightly Colonial in nature. Windows were often symmetrically placed on the front façade but not on the sides. Windows could be paired on the second floor and grouped into threes on the first floor.

The Foursquare house was nearly always divided between floors on the exterior by some form of trim board. This division was not always at an equal point between the top and bottom, with some homes showing approximately two-thirds first-floor and one-third second-floor division.

Sources of Foursquare Design

The Foursquare was an extremely popular housing type in the early years of the twentieth century. Stickley pictured several of them in his *Craftsman* magazine and Sears, Roebuck and Co. featured the house type on the cover of its first *Modern Homes* catalog in 1908 (fig. 49). In the house-plans and kit-house catalogs from 1900 to 1920, about 15 to 20 percent of the houses were Foursquares. Not all the Box Houses were covered in Arts & Crafts decoration. Some had Colonial ornamentation, while others had English Tudor detailing. Exterior surfaces consisted of the standards of the period—wood clapboards, sometimes very narrow; wood shingles; stucco, both rough and smooth; and cement. In most cases the surface materials were combined on a house with one floor built of a wood material and the other of masonry. Another common orientation was clapboard over shingle over stucco.

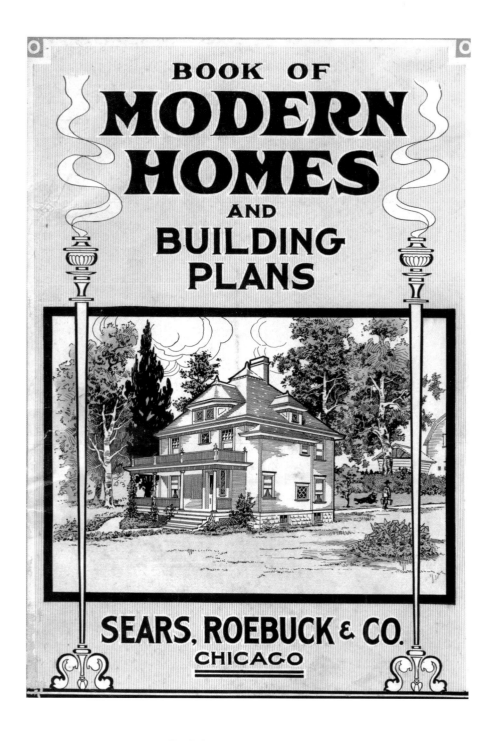

Fig. 49. Sears, Roebuck and Co. thought enough of the Foursquare style to feature it on the cover of its first *Modern Homes* catalog in 1908.

Foursquare Colors

Fig. 50. This large rectangular Box House, or Foursquare, provides an impressive canvas for exterior colors.

Four basic categories of color schemes were common for this type of house, based on a review of period literature. These include the single color with contrasting trim, the rustic stucco or cement-covered Prairie style, the basic two-tone, and the "Motif" color house. The single-shade models mainly relied on a colorful contrasting roof for additional visual interest. Homes such as figure 51 were built with a green shingled roof and window sash that contrasted nicely with the orange/yellow body and the off-white trim. A similar example features a terra-cotta body with sage green trim and a medium-gray roof. This type of color combination makes the house appear blockish and sturdy.

Fig. 51. An example of the single-body-color Foursquare home. The yellow-orange color coupled with a green roof was a popular combination around 1915.

Another popular type of Foursquare exterior was one that featured detailing and surfaces popularized by Frank Lloyd Wright and his Prairie School. Most of these homes were simpler and only hinted at the detail of the master architect. They were usually covered in a rough stucco or concrete surface. This material was often colored, either in the original mixing or by painting afterward in a light color such as tan, gray, or vellum. The trim was typically in a highly contrasting darker color such as olive or dark green. Such architectural details as belt courses or window trim would be in this darker color to dramatically highlight them. Figure 29 on page 52 illustrates this color scheme where the horizontal lines of the house are specifically brought to the viewer's attention. Figure 52 uses a two-tone colored concrete of tan and light orange with a green roof and off-white trim over a natural gray foundation to create a lighter example of the Prairie Foursquare.

The most common Box House scheme for coloration was two-toning, which was used to create a more horizontal illusion of the ground-hugging bungalow. In this category, the house façade is divided by a belt course between floors. One section is painted a dark natural color such as medium brown or green, while the other section is a much lighter color such as sand, light yellow, or off-white. The trim is usually painted in an even lighter color. Figure 53 has rustic stained-wood shingles on the shortened upper floor and light-yellow clapboards on the lower floor. A

Fig. 52. A Prairie-style Foursquare with minimal decoration, but a colorful exterior of orange, cream, gray, green, and white.

Fig. 53. An abbreviated second story in a darker color over a much lighter first floor creates the illusion of a short, ground-hugging bungalow.

Fig. 54. About 1915, Sears, Roebuck and Co. offered this lively example of a colorful Foursquare in a rural setting. Olive, orange, white, and natural concrete gray are combined under a rust-red roof into a striking scheme.

brown roof, white trim, and brown windows cap off the scheme. A Sears, Roebuck and Co. advertisement illustrates a more colorful version of the three-tone Foursquare, with an olive second floor sandwiched in between gray gables and an autumn-orange first floor (fig. 54). A natural gray concrete porch with white trim sets off this colorful example from about 1915.

"Motif" color schemes reflected a particular architectural style that was the overriding design consideration for the home. Figure 55 attempts an Arts & Crafts design with its red diamond details at the roofline and its high brick foundation with stark English-style stucco wall surfaces. The low-pitched roof in red tile provides an oriental touch. Some of the most popular motif color schemes harkened back to Colonial antecedents. The Colonial Revival style of architecture was popular in America from the

Fig. 55. A motif color scheme is illustrated in this Ideal Homes Plan Service Company offering from 1925. Note the red diamonds and quoins around the entry door.

Fig. 56. This Colonial-style Foursquare is enhanced by black window sash, cream trim, and an olive green body.

1880s through the mid-twentieth century. Foursquare designs could have Colonial features as well as those of the Arts & Crafts style. Figure 56 illustrates this with a rounded front porch in a cream color set off by the black window sash and light-olive body color. A green roof caps the house. This harmonious color scheme provides a soft, light feeling to the house.

Contrast was the typical design consideration for color combinations on Foursquare homes. One surface area was usually darker and one lighter, although the two areas could be the same color but in different values. The reason for the two-color scheme was to make the house look at if it were lower and closer to the ground. The darkest color was not always on the bottom, as logic might suggest. The most popular colors for Box Houses seemed to be naturalistic. Various browns, both medium and dark, were popular, as were darker greens, olives, and medium grays. During the 1920s, colors lightened with the introduction of yellows and tans. The masonry surfaces tended to be lighter than the wooden siding areas. White was not that popular, but off-whites, creams, and vellums were. Tints of light green, like sage, or light yellow could be painted over the stucco or incorporated into the mixing to achieve the color. Some Foursquare examples in catalogs do show the entire house in one body color, mainly dark, but those are relatively rare.

TRIM AND ACCENT COLORS

Trim colors needed to complement the body color. Often this led to trim areas that included eaves, window trim boards, and corner boards painted in a light or medium color to contrast with the darker browns and greens. In this instance white was acceptable but, more often than not, off-whites, creams, and vellums were used. Colors such as sage and light yellow, or slightly tinted off-whites with gray, green, or yellow were also in use. When the body of the house was in a medium or lighter color, the trim could be colored in a darker shade such as olive, dark green, or brown. The combination that best illustrated the trim and architectural features of the house were the ones most favored in the early decades of the twentieth century. These consist of an autumn palette of brown shingle siding over perhaps a light brown or green stucco, with the trim done up in cream.

Fig. 57. This Sterling Homes Senator B model highlights the low-pitched roof of the Box House, one of its most common and recognizable features.

Little details are often highlighted in Foursquare color schemes. Porch column panels such as the one shown in figure 51 on page 74 were showcased by either employing the body color or a completely different complementary color. Decorative moldings such as those on the front bay window in figure 29 on page 52 were also selected for color highlighting. The decorative porch stick moldings on the Sears, Roebuck and Co. farmhouse in figure 54 on page 75, as well as its side bay/oriel brackets, are another example of painted detailing. Exposed roof rafters at the eaves could be painted in a contrasting color as well. The idea was to show off some of the detailing of the house, but not in a fashion that resembled the more ornate and intensive color placement of the Victorian era.

ROOFING MATERIALS AND COLORS

Because the Foursquare house became popular a bit later than the bungalow, and because of its unique shape and configuration, the roof tends to be of less visual importance. Since bungalows were shorter, the roof was naturally easier to see and therefore more a part of the overall color plan. With a two-story house that mainly featured a short hipped or pyramidal roof, the color was less of a distinguishing feature. Like the bungalow, browns, grays, reds, and green roofs were popular on Box Houses. Green seemed to be the most popular choice, with examples shown in period sources that covered nearly all the tonal ranges from dark forest green through medium to lighter sage green. Reds and terra-cottas were also fashionable. Composition shingles were in common use on this class of house, as were tile and slate materials. It is important to note that the roof color was an integral part of the Foursquare color scheme even though the percentage of the visible roof was less than the bungalow. That being the case, colors such as very dark brown or black were not popular as they provided a rather somber cap to the house.

POSTMODERN ARTS & CRAFTS

Beginning in the late 1970s, advertisements began appearing in house plans magazines for the revival of a type of house not seen on the American landscape for nearly eighty years. Homes with towers, wide front porches, high-pitched gables, and decorative siding were being advertised as the newest fashion in house design. These "New Victorians" began a movement away from the prevailing styles of the late twentieth century—the Bi-level, the Colonial, and the Ranch. Home styles with some historical attachment were again in vogue.

Fig. 58. A modern Arts & Crafts home. While recently built, it has the look and feel of homes from the early twentieth century. (Photo provided by The Bungalow Company.)

Fig. 59. A Postmodern Arts & Crafts building that harkens back to its original English roots with large shingle siding, high-pitched gables, and outsized windows. (Photography: John Dimaio; Architecture: Fletcher Farr Ayotte PC, Portland, Oregon; Project Architect and Designer, Brett Schulz.)

Not long after modern Victorians began to be built in large numbers, house designers and architects rediscovered the buildings of the original Arts & Crafts period and employed them as inspiration for the next wave of fashionable new-styled homes of the late 1980s and early 1990s. These so-called Postmodern or New Modern bungalow and Craftsman homes drew their inspiration directly from the now-famous original homes of the early twentieth century. Leading the way were houses that looked like the Sears, Roebuck and Co. and Aladdin catalog bungalows and more-modern descendants of the larger Stickley-inspired Craftsman residences (fig. 58). This revival style not only included new single-family dwellings, but also vacation homes and condominiums. With this new style came a meshing of architectural details that included American Arts & Crafts as well as the English Arts & Crafts and Edwardian periods. We might call these homes "Traditional Arts

Fig. 60. With its clean stucco siding and wood-shingled bays, this new building in Portland, Oregon, seems to have been inspired by the works of British architect C. F. A. Voysey, proving that modern architecture can have style and grace. This building won a 2000 Portland AIA Chapter "Craftsmanship Award." (Photography: John Dimaio; Architecture: Fletcher Farr Ayotte PC, Portland, Oregon; Project Architect and Designer, Brett Schulz.)

& Crafts Reproductions." They tend to have features similar to their historic counterparts, including wide front porches, shingle siding, roof dormers, abundant windows, and pergolas (fig. 59).

While most Modern Victorians would not be mistaken for their nineteenth-century counterparts, the Postmodern Bungalow adheres much more closely to the original philosophy and has the look of an early-twentieth-century house. The modern homes are generally larger in size to reflect our current affluence and a desire for more square footage. Some new plans show large stucco surfaces reminiscent of English Arts & Crafts designs. A number of these new homes look as though they were taken directly from the pages of the many American house plans books available in the 1910s and 1920s. Examples are even taken from historic English architects like Voysey and Baillie Scott (fig. 60). The idea is to achieve the actual look and feel of an original Arts & Crafts home. Much of the overall massing, and especially details like doors, windows, and pergola porches, appear as nearly exact reproductions of the original designs from the pages of *The Craftsman* or similar publications. Siding materials are true to the earlier Arts & Crafts designs as well, with a wide use of wood or wood-like shingles. Windows are grouped in bands in a similar fashion to those homes built prior to World War I and have fenestration (divided lights) that copy period models. Some window designs are produced in colored-glass patterns similar to those developed by Frank Lloyd Wright for his Prairie-style homes.

A second group of these new Arts & Crafts homes might be labeled "Modern Traditional" for their incorporation of historical

Fig. 61. This high-styled Arts & Crafts Modern Traditional design incorporates elements from the old as well as the new. Craftsman eaves brackets and tapered porch columns are mixed with an attached garage. The color scheme is reflective of the mid-1920s.

Fig. 62. This newly built combination office and garage has many traditional features, including the wide overhanging eaves with exposed rafters, wide window trim, and a two-tone brown historic-period color scheme.

Fig. 63. Even more traditional plans can incorporate Arts & Crafts design elements, as shown in this house with its clipped gables and tapered porch columns. The second-story yellow is drawn from a historic paint brochure. (Photo by Steve Roberts.)

features and modern design elements. Houses like the one in figure 61 are constructed with shingle siding, eaves knee brackets, and an attached garage. Examples like figure 62 show a combination office and garage in the Arts & Crafts spirit. One other modern Arts & Crafts house type is worthy of mention. This home has a more basic rectangular-shaped plan and adds historic period detailing at the porch and eaves (fig. 63).

Postmodern Colors

The desire to capture the true essence of the nearly hundred-year-old Arts & Crafts home can be seen in the exterior colors of these new homes. Without a prevailing philosophy of color rules and with a much wider range of colors to choose from, these modern bungalows have more color options. Some strive for a look that resembles the earliest bungalows, including shingles stained in a medium natural color such as green, brown, or tan. These are generally monochromatic schemes and many have windows in white or off-white vinyl for their only contrast. Others have chosen to emulate the original English color schemes (fig. 64) with stained wood windows and colored stucco. Another popular scheme is a multicolored, pre–World War I type. These often consist of a medium body color, such as green, with contrasting darker trim, perhaps in brown, and with dark window sash in red. The lighter bungalow colors of the late 1920s with light trim are also popular. Entry doors are presented in the original fashion of stained wood. Some doors are reproductions taken from early-twentieth-century millwork catalogs and have the look and feel of a true Craftsman entryway (fig. 65).

Because of the limited variety of roof color choices in the late twentieth century, most of the Postmodern bungalows have either a brown or black roof. Recent advances in roof color and design have included the production of composite shingles that look like wood shakes. Some manufacturers are now offering a few colors such as dark red and green, as well as mixed blends of various shades to provide more contrast in the roof surface. Shingles with square and rounded edges, the classic wooden shake, and new tile and metal options are also available. While the variety of the early twentieth century is not available today, the current options do allow for a certain level of creativity in design.

As the Postmodern bungalow continues to be built in the twenty-first century, it will further evolve and builders will be able to take advantage of new technologies in construction materials and color.

Fig. 64. This complex of buildings includes an original Arts & Crafts home and new construction specifically designed and colored to harmonize with the old. The medium brown shingles, white stucco, and darker brown shingles with natural wood windows all work together in a complementary fashion. (Photography: John Dimaio; Architecture: Fletcher Farr Ayotte PC, Portland, Oregon; Project Architect and Designer: Brett Schulz.)

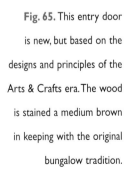

Fig. 65. This entry door is new, but based on the designs and principles of the Arts & Crafts era. The wood is stained a medium brown in keeping with the original bungalow tradition.

"We shall find aid in our problem in the simple, restrained color schemes found in the better Japanese color prints. Here we have colors of the utmost subtlety combined frankly with that delicate appreciation of the intimate relation of tones which is the despair of the Occidental decorator."

HARVEY ELLIS, "A NOTE ON COLOR" IN THE CRAFTSMAN, NOVEMBER 1903

Remember when you were in kindergarten or first grade and you had a package of twenty-four brand-new crayons and a blank piece of paper? Your "works of art" were lovingly placed on refrigerators or framed and hung on the walls. You didn't agonize over whether one color looked right with another; you instinctively put colors together in pleasing harmonious groupings. Sometime during your growth into adulthood, you lost that ability to automatically choose color. In order to regain that confidence, you will need to approach the study of color from a theoretical or structured format.

But don't worry! The concepts are easy and the language is simple to use. Start slipping these terms into your conversations and pretty soon your friends will be coming to you to consult on color choice. The first device to work with is the color wheel. It was initially devised by Isaac Newton around 1704 and subsequently refined by other color theorists. The wheel is divided into twelve equal slices or hues. Hue and color are two terms for the same concept. Red, yellow, and blue are considered **primary colors** or hues because you need some combination of these three to create all the other colors. They cannot be created by mixing other colors together. They are placed equidistant apart on the circle. Next come **secondary colors**. Purple, orange, and green are created by mixing two primary colors together: primary colors red and blue are mixed to make purple, red and yellow create orange, and yellow and blue yield green. The secondary colors are placed on the color wheel equidistant between the two primary colors that create them. Each **tertiary color** is created by combining a primary plus a secondary color. If you select red plus purple, the resulting combination is red-purple. See how simple this is? And you can also guess just exactly where they are placed on the color wheel—between the two colors that are blended together to create them. The other five colors on the wheel are blue-purple, blue-green, yellow-green, yellow-orange, and red-orange.

When you look at the color wheel, you can see that half of the colors are cool and the other half are warm. Your color combinations can stay completely in a single temperature zone or cross over the two. You need to decide when you look at your home and the landscape around it whether it would look better in cool colors, warm colors,

or some combination of each. Your location in the United States, or even in the world, also has some bearing on which may be the better choice. Typically, homeowners in states with warmer temperatures choose warm colors, and those with lots of snow choose cool colors. Of course, for every rule there are always many exceptions! You may want to start with your favorite color, which could dictate subsequent choices. When you select a color scheme with some cool and some warm colors, you will see that the cool colors tend to recede and the warm colors tend to advance or dominate. If you have areas that you want to highlight, warm colors, by their very nature, will help do that automatically.

One reason to use the color wheel is that some time-tested color combinations can be chosen just by looking at where the colors are located on the wheel. The first principle deals with complementary colors. If you select any primary color (red, yellow, or blue), the color directly opposite is a secondary color (purple, orange, or green), which is known as the complement of the first. What do you see when you look opposite red? The color is green. Just think about how frequently you see that pleasing combination, particularly in the month of December. It's not just chance that caused those two hues to be used together so frequently. Another little tip to know about complementary colors is that mixing the two of them together produces brown. If brown is one of the colors you want to work with, knowing whether it is yellow-brown or red-brown will help in paint selection.

A third facet of complementary colors is that you don't always use the same proportions of each color, according to Johannes Itten, a Swedish color theorist. For instance, red and green are equally intense and so they can be combined in equal proportions. However, blue and orange are different in value and so five parts of blue are most pleasingly combined with three parts of orange. In other words, orange is a more intense color and needs to be used a little more sparingly. When we get to the third combination, purple and yellow, these proportions become even more skewed: six parts of purple for every part of yellow. So remember that a little bit of yellow (depending on its value) may go a long way, and you won't need much yellow to provide excellent contrast and focal point (see fig. 80 on page 107).

A second rule of color choice deals with **analogous** colors. These are colors next to each other on the color wheel. Although this may seem almost obvious, red, red-purple, and purple work together very well. Any two, three, or four colors will provide you with a color combination that is pleasing. The difference between a complementary color combination and an analogous combination is the amount of contrast. The first provides a maximum amount of contrast, while the second is more subdued and subtle. Both can be good choices, depending on the house and the landscape in which they are going to be used (see fig. 42 on page 66).

Any standard geometric shape can be superimposed on the color wheel to create a **harmonious** combination. An isosceles triangle, when placed on the color wheel, would point to two colors that are separated by a single color (for example, yellow and orange) and a third color that is directly opposite the color between them (blue-purple). You will notice that two of the colors are harmonious and the third provides maximum contrast to both of them. This rule combines the best of both the complementary and analogous situations. Look at the color wheel and devise several other combinations with geometric shapes such as an equilateral triangle, a square, or a rectangle. These forms can be used to identify combinations that provide differing levels of contrast.

The color wheel is made up of colors in their purest form or intensity (fig. 66), but we know that we can select from thousands of different values when we are choosing paint or fabric. Just go to the paint store and look at all the paint chips. Some colors are lighter and others are darker than the pure color. Lighter colors, or **tints**, are made by adding white to the pure color. Darker colors, or **shades**, are made by adding black to the pure color. **Tones** are created by adding grey to the pure color. The values of the colors that we choose also maximize or minimize contrast. A navy blue used with a pale peach provides much more contrast than that same navy blue with dark rust. There are two levers that can be used to control contrast. One is the color or hue itself and the other is the value selected, from a light tint to a pure color to a greyed tone to a dark shade.

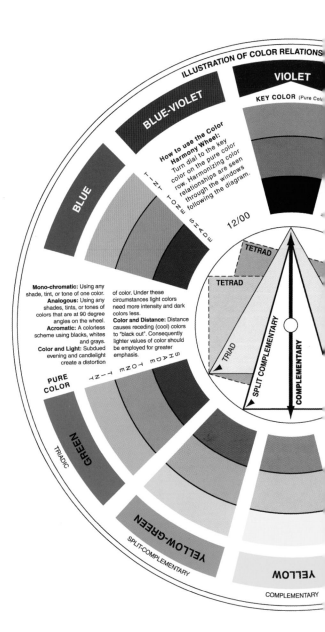

Fig. 66. Color wheel. These handy devices are available at artist-supply stores and via the Internet. (Image supplied by The Color Wheel Company.)

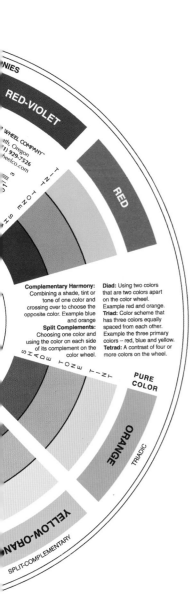

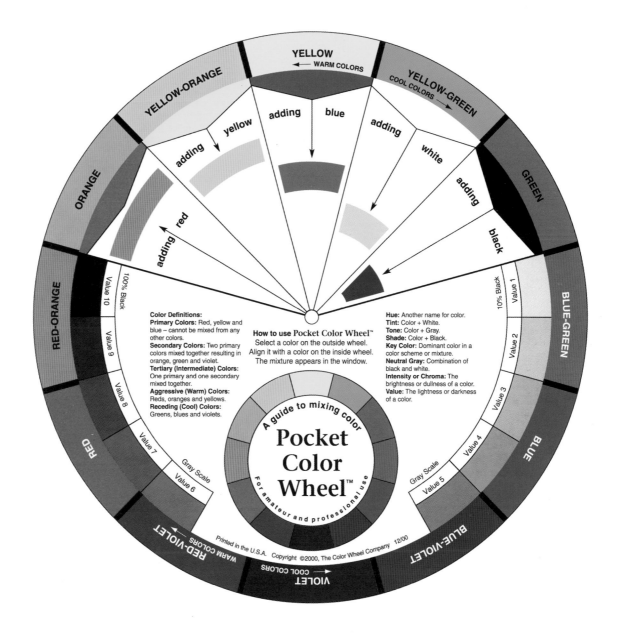

When choosing colors to be applied to buildings, many of the selections are tones with some amount of grey in them. Grey allows us to bring down the intensity of the color so that grass green becomes olive, or sunshine yellow becomes gold. Because exteriors are so large and have such visual impact, we typically choose greyed colors to soften the overall contrast (see the "after" photo on page 174).

Now that we know what creates the different values of a color, it's time to learn a few final terms. **Monochromatic** color schemes occur when you use different tints and shades of a single color (see fig. 81 on page 108). You might select two, three, four, or more different values of green in painting your house, from trim in the darkest evergreen to a body in pale celery with several other green choices in between. **Polychromatic** color schemes, like the complementary, analogous, and geometric ones described above, occur when you use two or more colors or hues (see fig. 77 on page 106). These schemes tend to create more visual excitement and interest than a single color. They are not quite as "safe" as a monochromatic scheme, but the risk pays off because of the interactions between the various hues.

Applying these simple color rules and employing a color wheel are excellent tools to assist in developing a pleasing house color scheme and avoiding costly mistakes. Add this information to the historical color data presented elsewhere in this book, and you have a much greater chance for success in your house recoloring project.

ORIGINAL SOURCES FOR COLORS

"The construction is stucco on brick, with roof of flat tile, the round pillars and the cross-beams of front porch and side pergola being of wood. This affords not only variety of material but also an opportunity for an interesting color scheme. For instance, if the stucco is left in its natural grayish tone or tinted a pale buff, the door and window trim may be a moss green with white sash, and the pillars and beams of porch and pergola either white or green, while for the roof, moss green or terra-cotta would be most in keeping. An effective touch of red brick may be added in the steps and as a border around the porch floors."

DESCRIPTION OF HOUSE PLAN, THE CRAFTSMAN, OCTOBER 1914

Unlike owners of nineteenth-century homes, the owners of bungalows, Craftsman, and other Arts & Crafts–era residences have a wide range of original historic period material on color available to them. This is true for two reasons. During the Victorian period, the process for printing in color was just emerging. The costly new technology could not reproduce colors accurately until around the turn of the century. Those few items from the period produced in color, such as paint company brochures, flyers, and magazine illustrations, are scarce today. Most of the ephemera has been destroyed or squirreled away in archives or private collections. Those items that do appear on the market today fetch high prices far beyond the reach of most homeowners.

At the turn of the twentieth century, several factors contributed greatly to the increase of the visual materials we use today to determine historic period color schemes. First, in the 1890s, a number of shelter magazines started publication. These were periodicals devoted to building, owning, and maintaining a home. Their number continued to increase between 1900 and 1920. Some major examples that are still familiar names today include *Better Homes and Gardens, House Beautiful,* and *American Home.* These magazines provided a myriad of ideas for decorating and enlivening one's dwelling. They also provided a ready resource for home-supply companies such as paint manufacturers to showcase their products. They catered to a growing homeowner population that had vastly expanded in the first few decades of the century. With a booming economy and an enormous increase in white-collar office jobs for both men and women, the possibility of owning a home became a reality for many more people.

Second, the ability to accurately print in color dramatically improved with the invention of more precise printing presses. More types of printed matter, from elaborate brochures to advertising flyers to calendars and simple handouts, were available to paint companies to distribute to potential customers. Architects, magazines, house-plans services and kit-house companies could now produce catalogs, books, or periodicals with color illustrations.

Third, an efficient national distribution system was established in the late nineteenth century. By 1900 the rail system linked every major city and nearly every sector

of the nation, and could move goods to virtually anywhere in the continental United States in only a few days. The rail system, coupled with the Rural Free Delivery Act passed by Congress in 1893, allowed catalogs such as those produced by Sears, Roebuck and Co. and Montgomery Ward to be shipped to any postal mailbox in the nation. People could also order paint from anywhere in the country and have it shipped to them, or they could purchase it locally at the growing number of local hardware stores.

These various "paper items" produced by a wide variety of sources in the early years of the twentieth century assist us in determining not only what colors were generally available to the public at any given time, but how they were used in the various architectural styles of the era. The most commonly produced informational pieces for paint are ones we all recognize today—the swatch chart and the fan deck. Swatch charts were provided to retail outlets to show available colors to customers, while fan decks were designed for professional painters and retailers. The swatch chart was nothing more than a set of small rectangles of available paint colors the manufacturer offered for sale. Many of these contained actual painted samples in the printed brochure. This trend of displaying small swatches continues in today's brochures.

One excellent method of viewing potential historic colors is to glance at the materials produced by paint companies and see what they had to say about popular colors at different points between 1900 and 1930. While these items are more plentiful than Victorian-era brochures, they are still somewhat rare, so examples have been reproduced here to provide you with at least a general idea of what was available.

Figure 67, first published in 1904, is from the Monarch Paint Company and illustrates some of the popular colors during the early Arts & Crafts period. Shown are an evenly split number of light, medium, and dark colors. As displayed, the colors pictured consist of three yellows, four greens, two reds, three grays, and two tans. An Aladdin Homes paint swatch set from their 1916 Readi-Cut kit-homes catalog has a similar color mix to the Monarch sample, but includes more brown and gray examples, along with the introduction of orange (see fig. 15 on page 38).

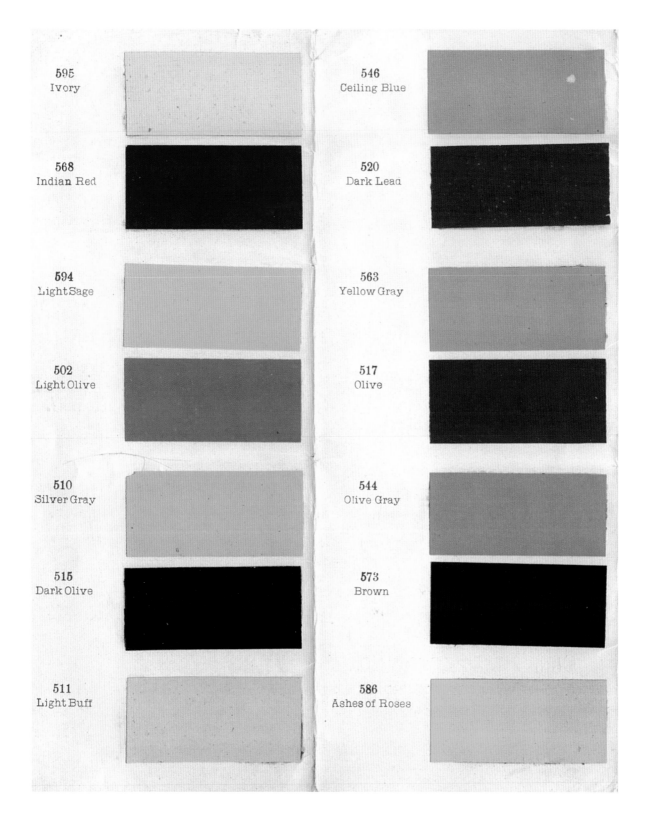

595
Ivory

546
Ceiling Blue

568
Indian Red

520
Dark Lead

594
Light Sage

563
Yellow Gray

502
Light Olive

517
Olive

510
Silver Gray

544
Olive Gray

515
Dark Olive

573
Brown

511
Light Buff

586
Ashes of Roses

Fig. 67. Monarch Paint Company exterior color sample from 1904. Note the general "autumn" look of the colors. This was in keeping with the Arts & Crafts philosophy on color design.

Fig. 68. Sears, Roebuck and Co. offered a large number of color choices in their Seroco Ready Mixed paint line. This is just one page from their 1916 catalog. The paint could be ordered and shipped via rail nearly anywhere in the nation.

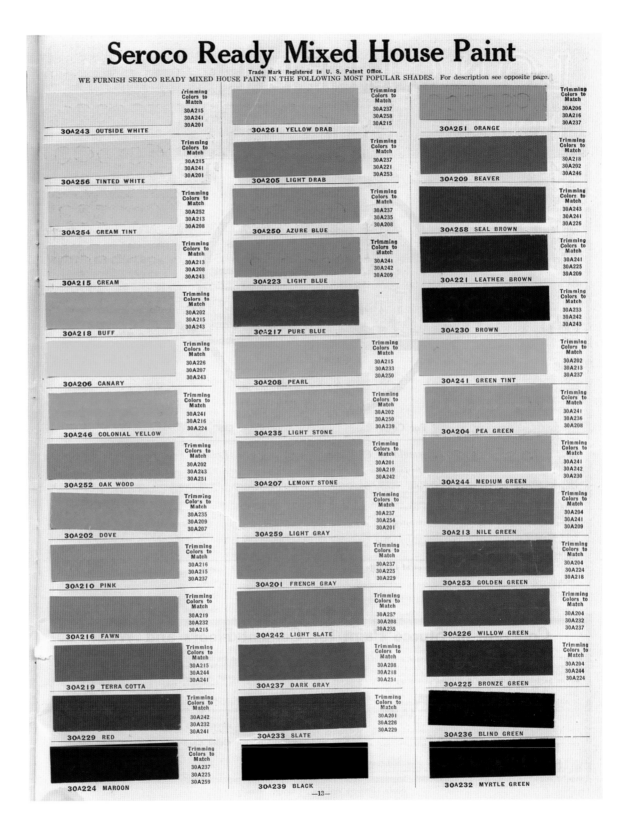

Seroco Ready Mixed House Paint

Trade Mark Registered in U. S. Patent Office.
WE FURNISH SEROCO READY MIXED HOUSE PAINT IN THE FOLLOWING MOST POPULAR SHADES. For description see opposite page.

Color	Trimming Colors to Match		Color	Trimming Colors to Match		Color	Trimming Colors to Match
30A243 OUTSIDE WHITE	30A215, 30A241, 30A201		30A261 YELLOW DRAB	30A237, 30A258, 30A215		30A251 ORANGE	30A206, 30A216, 30A237
30A256 TINTED WHITE	30A215, 30A241, 30A201		30A205 LIGHT DRAB	30A237, 30A221, 30A253		30A209 BEAVER	30A218, 30A202, 30A246
30A254 CREAM TINT	30A252, 30A213, 30A208		30A250 AZURE BLUE	30A237, 30A235, 30A208		30A258 SEAL BROWN	30A243, 30A241, 30A226
30A215 CREAM	30A213, 30A208, 30A243		30A223 LIGHT BLUE	30A241, 30A242, 30A209		30A221 LEATHER BROWN	30A241, 30A225, 30A209
30A218 BUFF	30A202, 30A215, 30A243		30A217 PURE BLUE			30A230 BROWN	30A233, 30A242, 30A243
30A206 CANARY	30A226, 30A207, 30A243		30A208 PEARL	30A215, 30A233, 30A250		30A241 GREEN TINT	30A202, 30A213, 30A237
30A246 COLONIAL YELLOW	30A241, 30A216, 30A224		30A235 LIGHT STONE	30A202, 30A250, 30A239		30A204 PEA GREEN	30A241, 30A236, 30A208
30A252 OAK WOOD	30A202, 30A243, 30A251		30A207 LEMONT STONE	30A201, 30A219, 30A242		30A244 MEDIUM GREEN	30A241, 30A242, 30A230
30A202 DOVE	30A235, 30A209, 30A207		30A259 LIGHT GRAY	30A237, 30A254, 30A201		30A213 NILE GREEN	30A204, 30A241, 30A209
30A210 PINK	30A216, 30A215, 30A237		30A201 FRENCH GRAY	30A237, 30A225, 30A229		30A253 GOLDEN GREEN	30A204, 30A224, 30A218
30A216 FAWN	30A219, 30A232, 30A215		30A242 LIGHT SLATE	30A252, 30A208, 30A235		30A226 WILLOW GREEN	30A204, 30A232, 30A237
30A219 TERRA COTTA	30A215, 30A244, 30A241		30A237 DARK GRAY	30A208, 30A218, 30A251		30A225 BRONZE GREEN	30A204, 30A244, 30A224
30A229 RED	30A242, 30A232, 30A241		30A233 SLATE	30A201, 30A226, 30A229		30A236 BLIND GREEN	
30A224 MAROON	30A237, 30A225, 30A259		30A239 BLACK			30A232 MYRTLE GREEN	

—13—

Sears, Roebuck and Co. was one of the largest paint suppliers in the nation in the early twentieth century. They sold paint through their merchandise catalog as well as through their *Building Materials* and *Modern Homes* catalogs. Sears also published a separate *Seroco Ready Mixed House Paint* pamphlet. The Seroco resource from 1916, shown in figure 68, contains one of the largest number of paint swatches of the period and contains several pages of small paint samples. They display a wide assortment of tones in typical color range for this period. For example, a single page from this publication illustrates forty-two available paint colors. This example includes nine greens, five grays, and four browns. It also shows four off-whites, three blues, and one pink. Another page presents examples of stucco paint in six colors. A Tower House Paints brochure from Montgomery Ward circa 1914 confirms the predominance of green and brown as popular exterior colors. This company's swatches also had a large number of medium and darker reds (fig. 69).

Because of their limited circulation, fan decks are rare but extremely useful color research tools. Since they were replaced regularly by the manufacturer, and retail outlets came and went through the period, most were discarded. The ones that survive provide a glimpse of larger color samples, usually on a thick stock, of the most popular colors from the World War I era. National Lead Company, manu-

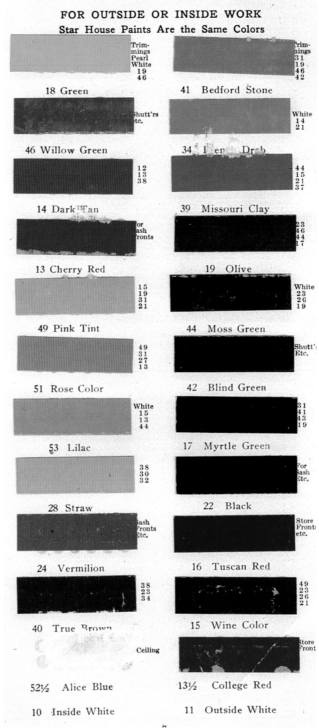

Fig. 69. Another major national paint supplier was Montgomery Ward of Chicago. This page, from their circa-1914 Tower Paints catalog, has some interesting choices, including pink, rose, and olive.

Fig. 71. Suggested exterior house color combinations from Monarch Paints in 1904.

facturer of Dutch Boy Paint, produced the fan deck shown in figure 70. It contains thirty-one colors in two-by-five-inch samples. The inside cover card tells us that "it is now possible to match the colors in this pack not only accurately but quickly." It goes on to describe the process by which these colors can be easily matched, thus eliminating guesswork from the mixing process. Each page of the fan deck has instructions for correctly mixing the exact color. For example, to mix a medium-tan color they call Drab #1006, the directions instruct you to "Match 1005 then add 4 lbs. raw umber." The dominant color in the fan deck is yellow, with seven different shades shown. Green, with six tabs, is the next most popular. Tans and grays are represented with five and three examples respectively, while white, olive, blue, and orange have one card each.

Once we have seen examples of period colors, we then want to know how colors were paired together. Historic examples provide several answers. First,

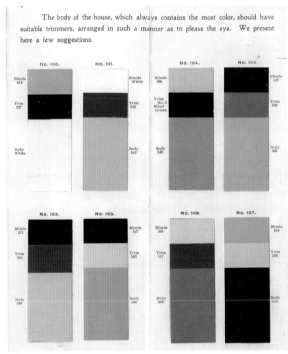

some paint companies published suggested combinations for potential clients. Figure 71 shows four possible options from the Monarch Company in 1904. They include three fairly light body colors (white, yellow, and sage), three medium colors in tans and browns, and two dark colors in shades of green. The suggested trims for these combinations are for the most part highly contrasting, with a dark green against the white, a dark brown against the tan, and a light tan against the dark green. The window sash suggestions also provide an additional visual contrast by adding a third color. These range from white for a sage body to red for a yellow body.

Another place where complete color schemes were shown was in advertisements for paint. Figure 72 from Montgomery Ward's Tower brand illustrates a yellow home with white trim and green shutters surrounding a dark window sash. A Sears, Roebuck and Co. advertisement for Seroco Paints illustrates five houses from 1914. The most prominent was an Arts & Crafts home called the Ivanhoe from their *Modern Homes* catalog, colored in two shades of brown and yellow. A bungalow in green and a Foursquare in two shades of yellow and olive are also pictured (fig. 73). The advertisement lists the cost of paint for each home, using two

Fig. 72. Tower Paints advertisement from 1914 showing a farmhouse updated with bright yellow paint.

Fig. 73. Sears, Roebuck and Co. employed this ad in 1914 for its Seroco Paint. It featured five homes in prominent period colors and hoped to lure homeowners to repaint in these new schemes.

coats, and ranges from $9.93 for the bungalow to $15.02 for the larger Craftsman home.

A Sherwin-Williams calendar provides us with further examples of complete paint schemes and exact dates for them as well. This 1902 publication illustrates five homes that highlight all the major architectural styles of the period. Among them is a Foursquare in a two-tone brown with tan trim and a bungalow with a terra-cotta roof, dark-green body, and yellow trim. Close inspection reveals further color-placement tips. The Foursquare's eaves have panels painted in a dark color to contrast with the light-painted exposed rafters. Also note the use of a separate color on the bungalow porch railings and spindles (fig. 74). These small examples show us what a national paint company thought were the best combinations.

Another source of period house color schemes is the small sample cards distributed by paint stores to customers. These cards illustrate various home types and suggest possible colors. A 1907 Lowe Brothers Paints card pictures a two-story Craftsman home with a brown body under a green roof with black window sash and cream trim. A darker cream is used as an accent color (fig. 75).

Sherwin-Williams also produced these cards. One set from around World War I has three interesting Arts & Crafts homes pictured. The first shows a two-story Craftsman (fig. 76) with a highly contrasting two-tone body combination—the first floor is white, the second dark green. The trim is a slightly different shade of dark green and the window sash is white. The wood-shingle roof is stained in a red-brown. The second card in the set shows another two-tone example with a terra-cotta upper floor over a light-tan first floor. The trim is off-white, and the roof is stained a medium green. The third example exhibits a sage body with terra-cotta roof and dark-brown trim. The window sash is yellow (figs. 77, 78). The backs of the cards offer two additional suggestions for color schemes.

Kit-house catalogs and house-plans books, especially after about 1910, began to show models in full color. Several of these examples help to illustrate the variety of color combinations available during the Arts & Crafts period. Sears, Roebuck and Co.'s *Modern Homes* catalog for 1912 shows a colorful Craftsman home on the cover. The model is pictured in two shades of brown with a green roof and upper story (fig. 73, center house). This home appeared in many Sears ads and brochures of the period. The Chicago mass-retailer pictured several models in

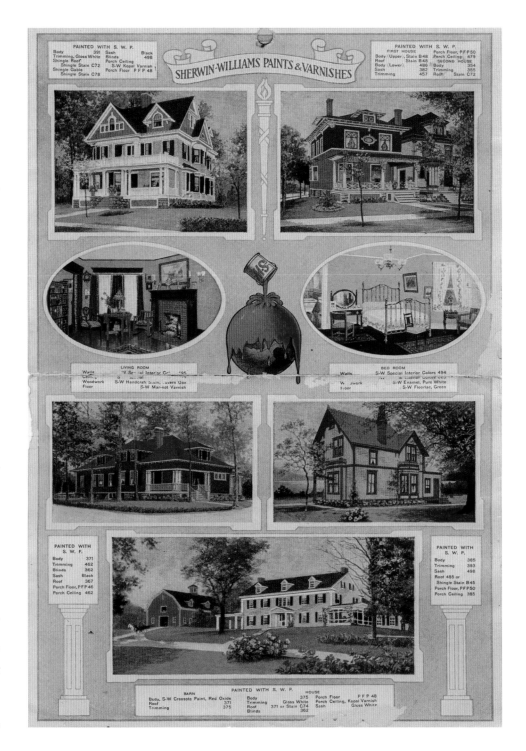

Fig. 74. A perfect example of popular paint schemes is shown in this 1902 Sherwin-Williams calendar. Since Sherwin-Williams was a leading paint manufacturer, their suggestions were likely copied nationwide.

Fig. 75. Sample color card from Lowe Brothers Paint Company in 1907. Illustrated is a Craftsman house with a brown-tone color scheme. Paint stores handed out these cards to potential customers.

Fig. 76. A Sherwin-Williams color card from around 1915. This example features a high-contrast, two-tone scheme of dark green and white.

full color in each annual kit-house catalog. The Argyle bungalow from the late 1910s illustrates a typical popular color scheme of brown shingles, off-white trim, and gray stucco surfaces with tan accents (fig. 79). Figure 80 is a Pyramid bungalow from Sterling Homes from 1919. Called the Winsom, this bungalow came in two sizes, 24 x 38 and 28 x 38, and is pictured in a medium-green body with yellow trim, a red roof, and black window sash.

Fig. 77. This Sherwin-Williams color card shows a Craftsman-style home in terra-cotta and tan with off-white trim. The green roof provides a stunning cap to an exciting scheme.

Fig. 78. This Sherwin-Williams example employs a lighter body with dark trim. The naturalistic color combination is typical of Arts & Crafts–era homes.

An excellent example of the changing taste in color schemes is shown in the Miracle model by Sterling. This house was a popular bungalow kit-home for the company, and it stayed in the catalog for many years while other model types were discontinued. Three examples (figs. 81, 82, and 83) illustrate the evolution of color schemes on one model. The earliest one, from 1914, shows the house in an all-brown scheme, in keeping with the prevailing fashion of darker, earth-toned colors popular in the early part of

Fig. 79. Some of the best exterior color images of the Arts & Crafts era came from Sears, Roebuck and Co. The stylish Argyle bungalow was one of the company's most popular models and was available from 1916 to 1926.

Fig. 80. The 1919 Winsom model from Sterling Homes is pictured with a bright green body in colorful surroundings and with a roadster in the driveway.

the Arts & Crafts era. Example two, from just after World War I, has a lighter body color of medium brown with off-white trim. This illustrates a trend of both lighter body and trims. The third example, from the mid-1920s, illustrates the same house in a yellow body with white trim, thus completing the transition from dark to medium, and finally to lighter, softer-looking schemes.

Some kit-house companies did not include color pictures in their catalog, but they did offer color suggestions for each house.

Figs. 81, 82, 83. The evolution of bungalow color is illustrated in these three examples of Sterling Homes' Miracle model. Beginning with a typically dark body in 1914, the shift to lighter color is evident four years later with a softer body and off-white trim. By 1920, the colors had shifted to even lighter shades, seen in the yellow body and white trim.

The Gordon-Van Time Company began to list colors in the late 1910s. Their 1923 *Fine-Homes* catalog lists nearly one hundred models for sale by mail. Home number 537 notes, "Unless otherwise instructed, we will furnish cream paint for the body, white for the trim and oxide red for the wall shingles of this home." Other models suggest "seal brown shingles and white trim" and "silver gray stain and off-white for the trim." The suggestion for a Foursquare house is "Clear Gray" for the lower body clapboards, green

Fig. 84. The 1920s saw a dramatic increase in color printing, especially in house-plans books and catalogs. This Prairie-style example was offered by the C. L. Bowes Company.

Fig. 85. This stucco home, from the book *American Homes Beautiful,* is tinted a soft green with highly contrasting dark brown trim. Books such as this were plentiful and illustrated many houses in color.

for the shingles, and white for the trim.

House-plans books of the later Arts & Crafts period are also an excellent source for color information. The price of printing color images dropped by the early 1920s, which could be seen by the increase of house-plans books with homes illustrated in color. The C. L. Bowes Company printed an elaborate hardcover plans book, nearly two hundred pages in length, called *American Homes*

Fig. 86. A Morgan Better Built Home model from about 1919 shows a shed-roof bungalow in a handsome green-and-white scheme. The red roof and brick foundation provide additional color.

Fig. 87. Olive and gray are not necessarily thought of as companion colors, but in 1919 they were paired with terra-cotta and red brick for a striking bungalow.

Beautiful. Bowes distributed the book through lumber dealers who sold the plans and the building materials. Every home featured in this book was shown in color. Because of the company's location in Chicago, there is a strong Prairie-style influence throughout the publication. Figure 84 is a typical two-story Frank Lloyd Wright–inspired design in a three-tone scheme. Thin, dark-green board siding is surrounded by gray stucco and medium-brown trim. A Craftsman-style home (fig. 85) is shown in light-green stucco with

Fig. 88. A truly autumn-palette Arts & Crafts color scheme is shown in this double-front gabled bungalow from about 1919. Orange and terra-cotta are framed by off-white trim and a dark green roof.

dark-brown trim and windows. One of the bungalows incorporates a two-tone body with russet top, medium-green bottom, and off-white trim.

The Morgan Company's *Better Built Homes* catalog from the same period illustrates similar homes in different color schemes. Bungalow Design 12430-A presents a shed-roof-style house with a white first floor, topped by a dark-green shingled second floor and a red and orange roof (fig. 86). Design 12597-A (fig. 87) colors a similar style of house in gray and olive with off-white trim. A double-front gabled bungalow, Design 12608-A (fig. 88), is pictured in orange and terra-cotta. With the ability to print more illustrations in an expanded range of colors, house-plan sellers often chose to show homes in a variety of color schemes rather than in a single, monochromatic design. The colorful illustrations throughout the books and catalogs served to show prospective home-owners not only the variety of models available, but also the range of colors for those models.

By studying these house-color examples and the paint-brochure color swatches, you can devise your own color scheme utilizing authentic Arts & Crafts–period colors.

"The siding is of redwood shingles, as is also the roof, and the masonry is of brick. The exterior color scheme is two shades of olive brown—a light-olive stain for the siding and a darker shade of olive for the trim, which, with the dull red of the brick, makes a most effective combination."

CHARLES ALMA BYERS, THE CRAFTSMAN, OCTOBER 1912

The process of selecting colors and combining them into an attractive scheme for your bungalow or Arts & Crafts home has been described in such terms as daunting, confusing, and even disturbing. Visiting a local paint store or home center may not simplify the task, as they offer thousands of stock colors, and an unlimited supply of custom choices beyond that. Confused homeowners often default to a "safe" color like white or taupe, from the sheer frustration of trying to pick appropriate colors, or else they just repaint their house in the same colors because they cannot visualize any other alternatives.

There is, however, a way around this dilemma. By following the guidelines and using the checklist below, you can create a new, exciting, and historically appropriate color scheme for your home that will be not only pleasing but unique as well. The suggestions below are based on years of research and my work in assisting hundreds of homeowners in developing their own color schemes.

STARTING AT THE TOP: ROOFS

One vital area of a home's color scheme that often goes unnoticed is the roof. Because it is not actually painted or stained, it tends to receive scant attention in the color design. Since you see it every day, it becomes so much a part of the house that you forget about it. As an experiment, describe the roof colors of the houses on either side of you. Don't be surprised if you can't. Homeowners are apt to worry more about the color of the front door than how their existing roof fits into their overall color plan. The results of this oversight can be disconcerting or downright unattractive. Drive through any older neighborhood and you will see buildings with gray roofs and tan siding, or brown roofs and blue siding, that stand out as examples of neglecting to consider all the elements in the design. This section is intended to give you the tools you need to analyze your roof and make sure it does not compromise your final color scheme.

Leafing through a turn-of-the-century Sears or Ward's merchandise catalog, you cannot help but be amazed at the variety of items offered for sale. This plethora of

consumer goods was even more astonishing to nineteenth-century homeowners, who had witnessed a dramatic rise in the variety of consumer items from shoe styles to roofing materials in the latter part of the Victorian age. America's industrial revolution provided the perfect environment for innovation, and no place better illustrated this than the building materials marketplace. While we tend to think of early bungalows as being rustic and having wood-shingle roofs, this is only partially true. There were literally dozens of types of roofing materials available in 1900, and even more by 1920. With a new bungalow in 1910, you could have wood shingles that could be stained or painted, as well as composition shingles in a wide variety of colors. In Henry Saylor's book *Bungalows,* written in 1911, he notes several available types of roofing materials. Slate and tile were suggested as viable alternatives, as well as painted tin or metal roofs. Saylor suggested staining a wood-shingle roof with a gray creosote, noting that it would last between ten and fifteen years. The author also suggested that homebuilders look closely at the new asbestos shingle for a roofing material. Although more costly than wood at the time, they were purported to last longer and were much less of a fire hazard. The asbestos shingle evolved into the modern-day composition shingle. Today we have mainly standardized composite materials for new housing and replacement roofing.

Knowing what you have on top of your house will point you toward a specific course of action. First, should you keep or replace the roof? It is always better to make this decision in concert with the color scheme building process rather than paint and then replace the roof in the following year or two. It's important to know exactly what you have on the top of your house before beginning to develop an overall color scheme. Start by going outside and answering some questions:

1) What color is the roof now?
2) Do you consider it an attractive color?
3) How old is it? . . . and obviously the next question,
4) Will it need to be replaced in the near future?
5) Do you want to wait until the old roof's life

cycle is complete before changing it?

6) What is the roof-covering material?

7) How many layers of roofing materials are on the house now?

8) How much roof do you see?

    a. Look at the house from all four sides.

    b. Look at it from across the street.

    c. Drive by and check what percentage of the house you see as roof.

    d. If the home is new, look closely at the plans and ask the architect to show you a model so you can check how much roof you are going to see.

The last consideration is another major factor in deciding the color scheme for your home. A roof that is large and prominent will have a greater effect on the look of the house, and thus the color scheme, than a flatter, less noticeable roof. What color you currently have will steer you toward some specific color options for the main body of the house, and lead you away from others. The larger the percentage of the roof that is visible, the larger importance its color will be. For examples of roofs with various degrees of visibility, see figures 38 (p. 61) and 44 (p. 67), for a less visible roof, figures 28 (p. 51) and 41 (p. 65) for a moderate amount of visible roof, and figures 42 (p. 66) and 52 (p. 75) for a large percentage of visible roof.

As you can see from the historic examples in this book, a wider range of color was used on homes in the early twentieth century than is used today. Luckily more roof-shingle manufacturers today are expanding their color choices. You will have a greater opportunity to acquire a historic-looking roof by shopping around. Real wood shingles are still available but, while impressive, they are costly and require relatively high maintenance. Metal roofs are making a comeback and are now offered in a range of colors suitable for Arts & Crafts–period homes. Composite shingles are the most cost-effective materials. There are a number that have shape to them, including ones that look like

wood shingles and ones that have rounded edges (fish-scale effect). While these are more costly, they do provide a handsome, historic look for your color renovation.

Roof Color

Knowing the color of your roof is invaluable to developing a good overall color scheme. The roof color leads you down a specific path to a body color and can aid in suggesting trim colors as well. Below are the standard roof colors and their positive and negative attributes, as well as some suggested body colors that work well with them.

BLACK

Almost never seen in the Arts & Crafts period because of its association with industrial buildings, black today is a popular roof color for no other reason than it is safe and neutral. Since black is the absence of color, almost anything looks good with it and it won't clash with the colors of the trim that sit next to it. One major problem, however, is that it tends to press down on the house, giving it a hard dark cap that can overwhelm the building. Black also provides no color in an area of the house that historic period designers often used to enliven color schemes. If you have a black roof in good condition, you pretty much have free rein to develop a color scheme based on the body color you desire. Any body color from medium brown to yellow to blue-green would look just fine against a black roof.

GRAY

Another modern color that rarely appears in historic Arts & Crafts roofs is gray. With this color, you are generally forced to exclude the brown family of body colors. You will need to stick with blue-greens, yellows, reds, and, of course, grays. While blue is a good companion color, it does not seem to have been used very often historically. Olives, tans, and browns are out, as they tend to look muddy or even clash with the gray. If little of the roof can be seen, then your color options widen (see fig. 58 on page 80).

BROWN

One of the most typical Arts & Crafts roof colors was a natural brown. It is part of the autumn palette so popular with period designers. Brown provides a natural, almost rustic flavor to the housetop. With a brown roof it is easy to use the more natural colors associated with the early Bungalow period, such as olive, dark green, and russet. It also works well with all the wood colors of the brown family. Brown is favorable when employing the lighter colors of the 1920s such as yellow, orange, and sage green. What brown excludes are grays and blue-greens. If the roof is dark brown, it might be wise not to select a white or nearly white trim, as the contrast between roof and house will become more noticeable (see fig. 33 on p. 55, fig. 53 on p. 75, and fig. 83 on p. 108).

GREEN

Popular in the Victorian period, green was also acceptable to Bungalow-era color designers because of its naturalistic look. It works with browns, yellows, and reds, and with light and dark body colors equally well. It provides a noticeable, colorful addition to a scheme and can be chosen in various shades from light to dark. Today green is viewed as an odd roof color, and is not often seen in subdivision homes or on the covers of most roofing brochures. But more and more manufacturers are beginning to realize that this versatile color has a place in American architecture and restoration. Green roof shingles are now available from many major manufacturers. Depending on the shade of green roof you have or will apply, you may need to adjust your body and trim colors accordingly. The two major tones are blue-green and brown/yellow green (see fig. 28 on p. 51, fig. 52 on p. 75, fig. 77 on p. 106, and fig. 81 on p. 108).

RED

Like green, red was a popular color choice in the nineteenth century. While not as common as green in Arts & Crafts period examples, it was still widely used. Its popularity was similar for the same reasons as green. It fit the autumn palette, served as an

additional color in the scheme, and complemented much of the fine brickwork then in use on bungalows. Today red is making a comeback. Several major manufacturers offer a variety of tones for restorers, and it is used occasionally on new housing as well. A red roof opens up browns, greens, yellows, tans, and olives as body color options. Even combinations that include blue-greens, grays, and whites can be effective with a red roof. It might be the most versatile of the choices, if one has the courage to use it (see fig. 35 on p. 57, fig. 54 on p. 75, fig. 78 on p. 106, fig. 80 on p. 107, and fig. 86 on p. 110).

COMBINATION COLORS

Some newer roofing options offer a mixture of colored shingles to form a blend, or combination of colors. This modern style provides the advantage of giving the homeowner several colors on the roof while providing an interesting visual look. The combinations start with a base color like brown or gray, with other colors added. The grays often have red and black added, while browns have green and tan. The overall effect is of aged wood shingles or perhaps of slate. This type of roof effect is slightly more expensive, but it is worth the effort to check out the various options (see fig. 82 on p. 108).

With the roof prominence and roof color information settled, you can move on to the second step of analyzing your foundation and masonry.

FOUNDATIONS

Even though this part of the building anatomy is not the most attractive and is often ignored, it is nonetheless an element to be considered in the house's color scheme. Because most foundations are mainly concealed with landscape plantings, they tend to be overlooked. The Arts & Crafts period heralded the trend of planting bushes and shrubs around the building foundation. In the Victorian period, most of the landscaping was placed far away from the edges of the house. It was not until the early twentieth century that books began to show more substantial landscaping around the house itself. Some homes only show a thin line of slab or basement, while others sit higher on a semi-platform basement. Similar to the work of analyzing your roof, the amount of foundation area you can see will determine its relative importance to the overall color scheme. First, go out and determine how much foundation you can see on all sides of the building. Next, determine what type of construction material was used, as this can influence your color decision. Some of the most common period foundation materials are brick, stone, historic concrete block, slabs, and cinder blocks.

Brick

Does enough of the brick show to be considered in the color scheme? Often basement brickwork is carried up to the porch piers and even the railings. Knowing the color of the bricks will allow you to choose complementary colors that don't clash. Brick has color tone just like other building materials, and it's important to match it to the colors for the rest of the house. If the brick is already painted, then you need to consider that color when developing the color scheme (see fig. 87 on p. 110).

Stone

Similar to brick, stone has a dramatic effect on the look of the house. The foundation stone on a bungalow or Craftsman house is often carried to the chimney or into the porch area. Since stone comes in a wide range of colors, it is a good idea to identify the major stone colors in use on your house. Then you can design your color scheme to work smoothly with all or most of them (see fig. 78 on p. 106).

Historic Concrete Blocks

The Arts & Crafts era corresponded with the development of machines that could produce concrete blocks with various masonry designs molded into them. These

machines could be purchased through the mail from Sears, Roebuck and Co. or rented locally. They allowed the owner to make their own masonry blocks in a variety of "faces" that resembled various types of stone or brick (see fig. 53 on p. 75, fig. 76 on p. 105, and fig. 78 on p. 106). Originally these blocks were usually left their natural gray concrete color, but over the years many have been painted. If that is the case with your blocks, then you need to add the foundation of the house to the plan when developing your scheme. Because these blocks were only produced from the late nineteenth century into the early 1920s, they are of historic significance and should be treated as such. Repainting the blocks gray is appropriate. Employing a dark color to visually hold the house to the landscape is also recommended (see fig. 76 on p. 105).

Slabs

Some homes were built on slabs or with crawl spaces that show only a thin line above ground level. Some bungalow plans had the siding materials, shingles, or clapboards coming down to just above the ground surface, showing little of the foundation. Stuccoed homes often carried that surface material almost to ground level. In these cases, you need to decide if you can see enough of the slab area to warrant coloring it. There is an increasing array of concrete stains and paints available today to handle that task (see fig. 79 on p. 107).

Cinder Blocks

Often used in modern Arts & Crafts homes with poured concrete or to repair an older defective foundation, this material can be colored to lessen its stark appearance. You can tint it in a dark shade of green, red, or brown, or even the house's body shade if it is a medium tone.

First, check the condition of the foundation. Even if you plan to leave the foundation untouched, it is best to check its condition. Mortar joints should be repaired, cracks sealed, and the cause of spalling of masonry surfaces investigated. If the foundation surface has been previously painted, look for any bubbling, blistering, or areas where the paint has not remained and investigate the cause of the problem. This may require professional assistance.

Next, decide what your course of action with the foundation will be. You can leave the foundation alone, color it, or remove previously applied paint. If your foundation is brick or stone that has been painted, you may want to return the surface to its original state. Removing the paint can be time-consuming and labor-intensive, but the results are often worth the effort. Another option is to repaint the foundation to resemble a brick color.

While you are considering your foundation color options and surveying its condition, be sure to make note of other important features attached to that area. Be aware of any basement windows, access doors, and/or exterior steps, as well as storm cellar entrances. These objects will also need to be colored and should be part of any inventory of items you plan to paint. Once you have evaluated the building's foundation and made your decision about its color future, you are finally ready to move on to the major color decisions.

CHOOSING A BODY COLOR

There is a sad inclination today to just recolor a house in exactly the same colors it currently has. This propensity not only takes away any creativity from the process, but also leaves you at the mercy of the previous owner or builder. The color fashions of the past few decades leave much to be desired. We live in an age of bland houses. You have likely noticed the "Taupe Town" subdivisions that hug our freeways, and the neighborhoods of all-white homes that dot our cities. Often it is not the desire to recolor a house differently that is missing, but a methodology to accomplish it. The sheer dread of visiting a paint store or home-improvement center and looking at the thousands of color swatches has frightened more than one homeowner into "just playing it safe with white." What to do? This author, as others who have gone before me, suggests that you shy away from the prepackaged sets of colors offered in paint-company brochures. They may seem attractive but were not developed with any specific architectural style in mind. They usually feature the most current "popular" colors, thereby nearly guaranteeing your scheme will be out-of-date soon. The information contained in this chapter should allow you to overcome the fear of choosing a body color and get you on your way to a visually attractive home.

First, determine how many body colors your home will have. Many bungalows and Arts & Crafts–era homes were two-toned or even tri-colored on the body sections. Most houses have a divider line of trim or a siding change between floors or color areas. Take a close look at your house for those lines of demarcation. Review the original source pictures in this book to see how builders and paint companies illustrated single-tone, two-tone, and tri-color homes. If you are uncertain whether you want a multicolor body scheme,

develop color choices for a single body color as well, just to be on the safe side. (For single-color-body examples, see fig. 56 on p. 77, fig. 78 on p. 106, fig. 83 on p. 108, and fig. 84 on p. 109. For two-tone-body examples, see fig. 47 on p. 69, fig. 53 on p. 75, fig. 76 on p. 105, and fig. 77 on p. 106. For a tri-color-body example, see fig. 54 on p. 75.)

Second, pick one family of colors to start with. Perhaps yellows, greens, or browns are your instinctive favorites for the body. Acquire several paint and/or stain brochures, sample cards, or even entire fan decks from several manufacturers. Try to get a representative range of values from light to dark, remembering that the sample chips occasionally look nothing like the final product on the house. Now pick a second family of colors and repeat the steps. Narrowing your options at this stage helps you focus on what you think you might like specifically. It also keeps you from wandering all over the map trying every possible color.

Third, decide on a "look" for your house. A "look" is another way for you to narrow down your options and keep you focused. Below is a short list of some key words that describe this concept. These are not defined, as they should be used just to conjure up an overall image of the house. The look can be your checkpoint as you move throughout the process, assisting you in making your decisions. For example, if you want your house to look classy and you are considering a peach trim, you might decide that peach won't give you the look you desire and that a dark green might better serve the purpose.

Some possible looks:

- Bold
- Dramatic
- Elegant
- Traditional
- Cool
- Urbane
- Dynamic
- Folksy
- Luxurious
- Energetic
- Dreamy
- Earthy
- Historically correct

Fourth, start narrowing down the alternatives. Pick about a dozen colors from each color family that you might like to try. Then review your favorites and discard some. Try to end up with four to six colors to strongly consider. Keep them around for later comparisons in case your shortlist turns out to be too light or too dark. Do not look at the paint samples under incandescent light. The best place to review your colors is outside in natural light, at various times of the day (morning, noon, and evening). Some colors will look radically different depending on the light. The best approach I have discovered for making the final color decision is to test-paint the colors you are seriously

considering. Paint or stain some boards, or even color a section of the house itself. The quarts of paint or stain you purchase are little insurance policies against a costly larger mistake. It is very important to actually see the colors you are considering on a larger scale. The difference between a one-inch paint chip and a 4 x 8 sheet of plywood can be unbelievable. The difference between that same one-inch chip and the side of a house can be shocking. This is not something you want to rush through. The cost of hiring a painter today is cause enough to suggest you have your color selections firmly in mind before the crew arrives and starts recoloring your house. When viewing your test-painted boards or area, be sure to check the body color against the roof color and any masonry you are not planning on painting. View the samples at the times of day when you normally see your house. For many people, the times when you are leaving for work and returning home are considered the best.

Fifth, decide from the beginning who is going to play a major role in the color-decision process. Will it be all the family members? Do you include neighbors and relatives? Remember to please yourself, as you will be viewing this new look every day. Perhaps your aunt who loves powder blue is not the best person to ask for advice. Next, take some notes on your reactions to the various colors and possibly have a family discussion about your thoughts and reactions. Some people use a scoring method for narrowing their choices. Each person is allowed three picks, with first place getting 10 points, second 5, and third 3 points. This works well in large families. Decide if you have an outstanding "winner." Does the body color you have chosen give you the possibility of achieving the "look" you desire? Decide if you want to go to the second color family and repeat the steps. Live with your final decision for a few days, and don't give up on the process. Set a time limit for coming to a decision, but give yourself the luxury to stretch your deadline just a little. It's always better to be safe than sorry.

Sixth, once you have come to a decision, stick with it. Remember that you have followed some time-tested methods for selecting the body color(s). You have spent considerable energy and time. Make the decision and move on to the trim and accent colors.

Trim and Accent Colors for Architectural Details

While the body color sets the stage and provides the background for your new color scheme, it is the trim and accent colors that define the final product. The work you put into selecting body colors can be spoiled by skipping over or taking too lightly the finishing touches. As opposed to Victorian-era homes that have a plethora of gingerbread woodwork, most Arts & Crafts–period homes are far less ornate. That does not mean to say that they are devoid of architectural detail; they are just calmer and require a finer eye to highlight. What colors you choose to fill out the new color scheme, and just as importantly where you place them, will have a major effect on how successful your house transformation will be. In viewing the examples of period homes in this book, you can get a fairly good idea of what colors were employed as trim and accents and approximately where they were applied. If you are attempting to achieve a truly historical look, they provide an excellent guide. However, if you are looking to enhance the architectural details of your home with color, these images may not be the best source of information. For one thing, the printing process in the early twentieth century did not allow for very detailed images with small areas of color on them. This is why you see few examples with any detail coloring.

The large interest in nineteenth-century Victorian-era architecture and its modern reintroduction in the late twentieth century have given rise to a propensity to highlight nearly every detail of a house with a different color. This trend has spilled over onto the Bungalow-era homes as well, with more and more people accentuating architectural details with color. Purists may consider this inappropriate, but there is historical precedent for it; and to the general public, highlighting is the perfect way to add visual interest and point out the interesting details of a house. (For examples of various methods of applying color to brackets, see figures 89–93.)

Fig. 89. Contrasting
roof-edge brackets. One method
to accentuate details and add
visual interest is to paint eaves
brackets in an accent color. In
this case, red was chosen to
highlight that detail.

Fig. 90. Harmonizing eaves
brackets. The most common
method of handling the colors
on these decorative brackets is
to paint them the same color
as the general house trim.

Fig. 91. Face-colored
brackets. Another treatment
for eaves brackets is to color
just the face in a contrasting
color, leaving the sides the
same color as the trim.
(Photo by Anna Blackman.)

The thing to remember about trim and accents is that they are usually small splashes of color against the backdrop of the body color or the masonry of the home. They are employed to outline the house and to highlight special features such as the window sash, roof rafters, and trellises. To finalize your trim and accent colors, first decide on approximately how many different colors you will want or need. Remember that some painting contractors charge extra for each color they apply. To make that decision, you may want to consult the checklist of architectural details below. By assessing your house against this list, you can compile a shortlist of possible areas you want to highlight and have them firmly in mind when you begin to consider the next set of colors.

Architectural Details Checklist

The items listed below all normally require a color different from the main body color(s). Determining how many of them you have on your house and to what extent you wish to highlight them will greatly facilitate your decisions regarding trim and accent colors. Normally, a building in the Arts & Crafts era had one major trim color, sometimes a minor trim color, and one or two accent colors. When you finish analyzing your house for

the amount and visual impact of these details, you can sit down and see how many colors it should take to highlight them.

TRIM MOLDINGS

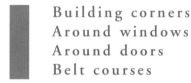

Building corners
Around windows
Around doors
Belt courses

Generally these areas have some type of surround molding. They were frequently considered by Bungalow-era designers to be trim and were colored in an appropriate manner. In the early years of the Arts & Crafts movement, they were usually a darker color than the body of the house. But beginning in the late 1910s, light colors, off-whites, and even whites were employed as trims. These moldings help outline the house much like a picture frame and should be treated as an important part of the overall color scheme. In many cases, the corner boards connect the eaves and the watercourse molding to form a distinct square outline of the house. If, over the years, your home has lost the lower watercourse boards, you can replace them or simply paint an area the same width as the other trim boards to reflect what would have been the molding. These trim areas were normally only done in a single color. If the moldings are thin and

Fig. 92. When brackets and rafters are visible at the eaves, their colors can be coordinated to highlight them.

Fig. 93. When the eaves and cornice area is a dark color, any brackets or rafters can be highlighted by employing one of the lighter colors in the scheme.

Fig. 94. This bungalow has contrasting trim that helps outline the house and define the window and door openings. Adding a contrasting trim frames the building and provides a specific outline for the house and its details.

Fig. 95. This Craftsman home has contrasting trim at the eaves, between the floors, and around the windows. This additional color helps make the transition from the dark upper story to the lighter lower floor.

Fig. 96. Rear and side doors were not usually stained during the Arts & Crafts period. These doors were often painted and had panels in an accent color as a highlight.

Fig. 97. This entry door is painted in an Arts & Crafts–period red that is employed as an accent elsewhere on the house, thus tying it into the overall scheme.

there is a general lack of other highly ornamented areas on the house, adding a second color to them is not advised (figs. 94, 95).

DOORS

Front
Back and side
Screen and storm

Most Bungalow-era homes have two or three doors. The main entryway door, or front door, was most often finished in a stained-wood color. However, because of age, deterioration, or replacement, the front door may need to be painted. The options here include painting it to look like wood, a medium brown for example; or, depending on the other colors in the scheme, choosing an accent color. Modern choices like burgundy and hunter green, seen in many new subdivisions, are inappropriate for the bungalow style. The rear door was usually employed by the family to access the yard and garage, so it encountered high traffic. The door was historically colored in a darker tone, but not the same color as the trim. Today it may have contrasting panels in a lighter accent color (fig. 96). Side doors, although rarer than the other two types, were also considered service entryways and treated in a similar fashion to the back door. With the Bungalow era came the mass introduction of

the wooden screen/storm door on both the front and back of the house. Typically they were stained in a medium to dark color, but painted examples do exist. Today's propensity for metal doors calls for the homeowner to decide if they want to go back to wood, paint the door they have, or leave it alone. If your storm door covers up a good deal of the inner door, then don't spend too much energy on detail-painting the inner door. If you paint the storm door, it can be the same color as the door behind it, but it can also be a complementary accent color (figs. 97, 98).

WINDOWS

Regular
Basement
Attic/dormer
Sunroom
Bay and oriel
Storm

With windows the first decision is to see if they are wooden and paintable or metal/vinyl, and/or how many of each category you have. The low maintenance of metal-clad and vinyl windows has made them a popular choice in remodeling historic homes. Sadly, replacing a set of vinyl windows is very expensive and not practical for a color switch. So, in some cases, you are left with white or off-white vinyl windows. If so, take that as a given and move on. Or should you? Some of the newer paint products on the market today claim to adhere to surfaces such as vinyl and metal, and offer hope that you could recolor the window sash. Consult your paint store and manufacturers' web sites or technical representatives for specifics (figs. 99, 100, 103, and 102).

Wood windows are easier to manage. Historically, especially in the nineteenth century, they were painted dark. This caused them to visually reside "inside" the house as opposed to a whitish sash that seemed to protrude from the façade. Bungalow-period examples show both dark and light window sash, although the lighter versions began to appear from the 1920s onward. The sash was usually a different color than the trim that

Fig. 98. The more typical Bungalow-era stained-wood front door is illustrated here. The use of natural wood was a hallmark of the Arts & Crafts philosophy.

Fig. 99. Windows are an important part of any Bungalow-era home because there were so many of them in this popular style. Generally, the sash was colored differently than the trim.

Fig. 100. This band of five windows is colored in a typical historical fashion. The sash is dark and the trim lighter to contrast with the body.

surrounded it, except in the case of very light sash. For the most visual impact, plan to have the sash a different color than the trim. Typically the sash was all the same color. If you have a mixture of window-material types, you must decide if you want to recolor the non-wood sash to match the rest, or vice versa. Basement windows were either colored the same as the regular sash or could be de-emphasized by painting them the same color as the trim. Roof-level dormer windows typically conformed to the color standard of the rest of the house, as did any sunroom windows. Bay and/or oriel windows likewise followed this pattern, with the siding matching the body color, the trim matching the corner boards, and the sash matching the rest of the house (fig. 101). Some color schemes, following a more Victorian style, have changed or added colors on these architectural features to further highlight them. Screen and storm windows historically were wood and colored to match the sash, or were painted in a black or very dark red. Today many homes are stuck with metal or shiny aluminum storms that detract from the overall color scheme. Again, you must decide what you can live with. If the storms stay in the windows all year, then painting them is a good option. If they are taken up and down a good deal, then the need for touch-up painting will be greater. Painting metal storms provides a cleaner look and

they are much less noticeable when properly colored. Some bungalow windows also have planters. These were usually painted the same color as the house trim (figs. 104, 105).

EAVES

Cornice boards
Cornice moldings
Roof rafters
Brackets

Most Bungalow-era eaves were painted the trim color to help outline the building. A dark trim provides a firm distinct line and a light trim much less so. A good deal depends on your body color(s). Since the trim is meant to contrast with the body, you need to decide what colors will give you a distinct "edge" or frame around the house. Some eaves areas have thin trim moldings at the edges and where the soffit meets the cornice. You need to decide if you want to highlight any of these. A good rule of thumb is that if the molding is thin and you can't see it clearly from the ground, then using a color different from the standard trim will not be effective.

Many homes of the period had some type of exposed roof rafter, either extending out from the edge of the house or incorporated under the eaves. In most cases these are not the actual roof rafter

Fig. 103. Sun porches were becoming more commonplace in the late 1910s and early 1920s. This example highlights the sash and the intervening pilasters between them while keeping to the overall color scheme of the entire house.

Fig. 102. This home is highlighted by black window sash, popular in the early years of the twentieth century, against contrasting white trim boards. On a small house, this is an excellent way to add visual interest.

Fig. 101. Bay windows were popular on all types of Arts & Crafts homes. These new vinyl windows are hardly noticeable, as they are surrounded by period-color dark trim.

Fig. 104. Flower boxes or planters were a common feature of Arts & Crafts homes. They helped bring the natural world closer to the family. Generally they were colored to match the trim of the building.

Fig. 105. Some planters had designs and brackets. These can be highlighted by using an accent color, as in this example where yellow is employed against an off-white background.

Fig. 106. It was common to have the roof rafters exposed on a Bungalow-era home. To highlight them without overemphasizing them, paint the lower face a trim or accent color.

ends, but are short special detail pieces added on when the house was built. In the early twentieth century, entire catalogs were devoted to just rafter ends. The question is whether you want to highlight them with a secondary color or not. The entire rafter or just the exposed face section can be colored. The same holds true for brackets. Many historic examples show them in the same color as the eaves but they are much more visual and perhaps more attractive when enhanced with an accent color. If you are unsure about coloring a bracket, try one out and then decide (fig. 106).

FRONT PORCHES

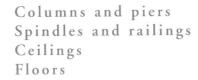

Columns and piers
Spindles and railings
Ceilings
Floors

The late-nineteenth-century Queen Anne Victorian–style house brought the large front porch, or verandah, into popular deployment on American homes. The Bungalow-era house continued this trend, but modified it to fit the simpler philosophy of the Arts & Crafts movement. Gone were the hundreds of ornate wood spindles and gingerbread, but remaining were the large and inviting spaces. Nearly every home built between 1890 and 1930 had a front porch. While

Victorian-era homes could have lavishly painted porches that carried three or four additional colors, the Arts & Crafts–era porch had its colors pulled from the rest of the overall scheme. Many homes had short columns, either round or squarish, on piers of masonry. These columns were often colored in a light tone but can be seen in some dark shades as well (figs. 107, 108, and 109). Often piers were of masonry. If they have been painted over time, then you need to decide if you wish to strip the paint, recolor it to look like brick or stone, or employ a house-trim color on them. Usually the columns and bases were different colors, so keep that in mind when choosing how to paint them. Some columns have moldings, capitals, and bases on them. These were not always highlighted in period examples, but do add visual interest when colored in a contrasting accent color.

Many porches have some kind of railing and spindles between the piers. These were usually treated in a simple fashion, either all the same color or with the railings being a darker color. The trim color was often used when the porch was a single color. With two colors in this area, the trim color was used on the railings with a complementary accent color on the spindles. A popular Arts & Crafts porch detail is the solid, short wall between the piers or in place of them. This type of construction became fashionable in the post–World

Fig. 107. Columns are an important part of the Arts & Crafts porch. This example colors the shaft in a traditional light color while highlighting the base and capital in different tones.

Fig. 108. Another column treatment is to color the base, shaft, and capital all the same, but highlight any decorative elements on the column in an accent color.

Fig. 109. This bungalow makes dramatic use of color in its porch columns. A terra-cotta was employed to provide a special accent to that architectural element, making it stand out.

Fig. 110. The space between the porch columns should not be neglected. This example shows how the rails can be a dark color and the spindles a lighter tone, highlighting that area. (Photo by David McKinney.)

Fig. 111. This Postmodern Arts & Crafts home has its railing and spindles in a dark color against the light posts and trim, almost making them disappear.

Fig. 112. Many Arts & Crafts homes had a solid wall on their porch or terrace. This example has a shingle-covered wall colored to harmonize with the upper story of the house. This provides an added bit of scale to the overall front façade, reducing the impact of the light-colored first floor.

War I era when auto traffic became popular and noise and fumes came to neighborhood streets. This detail was usually painted in the body color (figs. 110, 111, 112, and 113).

Bungalow-era porch ceilings were the first to make extensive use of installed electric-lighting fixtures. For this reason, the ceiling treatment fell into two categories. Ceilings could be colored in off-white to reflect the light downward, or they might be finished in a stained wood and varnished with a glossy surface. The Victorian technique of painting ceilings sky blue does not seem to have been followed by Arts & Crafts–era designers. Some ceiling areas contained exposed beams, and some contained beams and rafter ends. These can be highlighted by painting them the trim color with the panels behind a light color, or de-emphasized by painting them the exact same color as the ceiling.

Porch floors are a maintenance area to be seriously considered. Most original porch floors from this period were painted. Manufacturers provided specific lines of floor paint that were touted as wearing better than their regular product. The reality turned out to be an almost-yearly maintenance chore to touch-up or recoat the floor. Popular colors seem to have been dark grays, reds, browns, and greens that harmonized with the rest of the paint scheme. Today several options are available to address this issue, and you should

check the technical specifications for employing stain vs. paint with the manufacturer.

The color you choose for the porch floor does not have to correspond to the limited early-twentieth-century offerings from the paint companies. Today many people choose to color their floors in the trim color or a slightly different shade of that color, or by adding a completely different color just for the porch floor. Since this is an area visitors will regularly see, color harmony with the rest of the house is important. Homeowners with concrete porch floors should consider a concrete stain (fig. 114).

STEPS

 Front porch
Side
Rear

The various sets of steps used for entry into the house serve different purposes but are affected by weather and traffic in the same manner. Most Bungalow-era steps were made of wood, and most were painted in a similar fashion to porch floors. Not all step sets were treated the same, however. Rear steps were usually painted in the trim color for ease of retouching. Any side steps might have been in the color of the foundation-level material to obscure them, although examples are shown in the

Fig. 113. An example of a brick half-wall on a porch. The patterns in the brickwork provide a perfect place to add some visual interest by painting the inset areas a light color.

Fig. 114. The Bungalow-era porch was an important place. The floor was usually a dark color and, as in this example, the ceiling was stained wood. With the colors of the trim and sash added, it is a colorful spot from which to take in the world.

Fig. 115. Porch steps generally receive scant attention, but painting the risers and runners in differing colors adds greatly to this already-attractive bungalow porch.

Fig. 116. Side entryways are another area where details can be highlighted. Here, a thin molding is painted in the trim color and the stoop-cover brackets and moldings are matched to it.

Fig. 117. Modern decking can be a problem on older homes, but with some thought and the right colors, an attractive combination can be achieved.

major trim color. What the front steps looked like varied, depending on the color design of the porch. Some matched the porch trim, others an accent color, while still others were the color of the body. On occasion the risers and the runners of the steps were different colors for added drama. Some original porch steps were done in brick, some in stone, and some in concrete. If these have been painted, consider removing the paint. Concrete steps, either original or new, can be stained, although the originals would have been left in their natural color (fig. 115).

REAR AND SIDE STOOPS

Often simple covers were placed on side and rear entries to provide protection from the natural elements. These normally simplistic, functional stoop covers should be colored accordingly. Using the major trim color on most of the pieces will work well. Any rafter tips or brackets can be

painted to match the eaves and/or porch coloring of those same items; however, that is not necessary. The colors on these items should not detract from the major architectural elements of the house (fig. 116).

MODERN DECKS

Many homes of the early twentieth century have been updated with a modern wooden deck in the suburban style. The major problem with these decks is that they are usually out of scale with the house itself and coloring them can often emphasize that fact. Try to strike a balance between the weathered, pressure-treated wood look of leaving them unpainted, and the heaviness of having that mass in a dark color. Stain is often a good choice for this area, and a medium shade with some tint that suggests the colors of the house usually looks good. Some paint companies make stains in popular historic colors, so it is possible to get a fairly close match to colors already in use on your house (fig. 117).

Review the checklist, organize the areas that need color, look at the definitions of trim and accents below, and decide on the number of colors. You may come up with something similar to this:

Outline trim—one choice, color #1
Window sash—one choice, color #2
Accents—two choices (brackets, porch spindles,
    moldings, doors), colors #3 and #4

USEFUL DEFINITIONS

While each house is an individual case and needs to be examined in detail for specific color placement, some general rules apply. The terms below generally define what we mean when we talk about what color goes where in your color schemes.

Major Trim—Usually this is a contrasting color to the house body. It is placed on corner boards and gable-trim boards of the house. It helps define the line of the house. It can also be used on porch railings and steps. Window-trim boards (not the sash) can likewise be in this color as well as trim around doors.

Minor Trim—This color is employed on doors, porch parts such as posts and spindles, and decorative trim that is part of or next to the major trim color.

Sash—This is defined as the part of the window that opens or moves. In a double-hung window, for example, it is the sections with glass that raise and lower.

Accent(s)—This term implies extra colors that are used to highlight special architectural parts such as brackets, porch posts, doors, and trim and accent boards.

How to Pick the Right Trim and Accent Colors

Once you have completed the checklist and decided how many colors you might like to use, how do you choose them? What colors go with what other colors is often a debatable issue. What we today view as unsuitable combinations show up in historic period sources as popular combinations. Some general rules can help guide you through the process of picking trim and accent colors to work with the body color you have chosen.

First, try for some contrast. Using dark colors for the body and trim diminishes the overall effect of both. Using a stark white, however, might be too much contrast. Arts & Crafts homes are known for their softer look, so try for something in the middle range with some, but not too much, contrast. Take a look at the examples in this book and you will see many illustrations of period homes and the visual recommendations made for trim and accent colors. Make a list of your favorites and discuss the reasons why you like each one. Examine the color wheel and see what colors work with the body color you have chosen. Look at homes similar to yours in the area and see what they have done. But don't try to adapt a Victorian or Cape Cod color scheme to your Arts & Crafts home; the scale of the buildings is different and the areas for color differ as well.

Some of the most popular color combinations are as follows.

Fig. 83.

Body: light to medium yellow

Trim: white or off-white

Sash: white

Fig. 53.

Lower body: light tan

Upper body: medium brown

Trim: off-white

Sash: bronze

Fig. 45.

Body: medium gray

Gables: dark green

Trim: white or off-white

Sash: white

Fig. 44.

Lower body: medium yellow

Upper body: medium brown

Trim: white or off-white

Sash: dark brown

Whatever combination you decide on, be sure to test it. You can paint thin stripes on your test boards next to the body color for comparison. The trim and accent colors show up in much less mass than does the body color, so view it proportionally. The major trim test area should be slightly larger than the accents or the window sash color. Or you can paint some sections of the actual house to get a feel for how the colors work together. This is an important step and should not be overlooked. See how the colors look with the roof and any masonry on the house. You may need to adjust the colors somewhat once you see them all together. If you set about making changes to the scheme, take notes on why you are doing so. This will keep you from an endless set of minor adjustments that only delay the final painting. Just as with the body color, involve your family and stick with your decisions. Once the color scheme is selected, live with it for a few days. Call several painters, get some estimates and references. Check out those references and set a start date.

Fig. 30.
Body: dark green
Trim: medium yellow
Accents and sash: white

Fig. 46.

Lower body: tan

Upper body: medium green

Trim: medium brown

Sash: cream

Fig. 43.

Lower body: white

Upper body: dark green

Trim and sash: white

Eaves: terra-cotta

This chapter showcases Arts & Crafts homes that have been transformed into historically accurate models through the use of color. All houses feature paints from Sherwin-Williams. In addition to identifying the paint schemes used on each house, two alternate color schemes have been suggested for each home.

Author's note: These suggested paint colors are not a panacea. They should be tested against the roof color and masonry of your house for compatibility. The color of neighboring houses as well as your landscaping should also be taken into consideration.

BONDS BUNGALOW

Empire, Michigan

Body: Downing Stone

Major trim: Rookwood Dark
   Green

Minor trim: Chelsea Gray

Accents: Downing Straw

Original Colors:

A common color scheme for many types of houses is a white body and sharply contrasting trim, in this case a dark green. None of the architectural features of the house are highlighted.

Desired Look:

To make the house look less austere and bring it more into harmony with the landscape.

New Colors:

The body is softened in an Arts & Crafts gray, and the trim remains green but less stark. Many features of the house once lost are now revealed with the use of yellow and gray accents. The gray paint and stone used on the house appear to change colors, depending on the sun, shade, time of day, etc. The house can look mint green and appear to be medium gray a few hours later.

Alternate Color Schemes

Body: Roycroft Brass
Major trim: Blonde
Minor trim: Roycroft Vellum
Accents: Copper Mountain

Body: Nomadic Desert
Major trim: Cardboard
Minor trim: Roycroft Bronze Green
Accents: Pacer White

GREENGUS CRAFTSMAN

Cincinnati, Ohio

Body, stucco: Natural

Body, shingles: Herbivore

Trim: Renwick Olive

Window sash: Polished Mahogany

Accents: Cupola Yellow

Original Colors:

The heavy, dark-brown upper story seems to dominate the front façade. There is a great deal of contrast between the two floors and none of the fine details are visible.

Desired Look:

To have the house look like it would have looked when it was built. Also, to lighten the second floor and emphasize the many architectural features of the home.

New Colors:

Color ideas included white on the lower section and brown or taupe on the upper shingles. Once the color tests were underway, green became the favorite; this turned out to be a lighter color than the previous brown. Instead of white, some color was added to the lower floor. An olive accent that complemented both floors was employed to tie the many diverse elements of the house design together. Awnings that match the colors of the house add additional visual interest. Note the color highlighting on the chimneys.

Alternate Color Schemes

Body, stucco: Whole Wheat
Body, shingles: Mossy Gold
Trim: Umber
Window sash: Rookwood Dark Red
Accents: Birdseye Maple

Body, stucco: Chamois
Body, shingles: Secret Garden
Trim: Blonde
Window sash: Renwick Olive
Accents: Rookwood Brown

KALIN/RICCIUTI BUNGALOW

Arlington, Massachusetts

Body: Birdseye Maple

Major trim: Fjord

Window sash: Rookwood Red

Accents: Creamy White

Original Colors:

A simple tan with white trim and a blue door make this double-front gabled bungalow seem quite plain and undistinguished.

Desired Look:

The owners thought the house was too light and looked too much like a Colonial. They wanted it to resemble a period bungalow.

New Colors:

Body colors considered were olive, brown, and gray. These seemed too somber, so a period maple-yellow body with blue-green trim was employed to enliven the house. The window sash is now highlighted in red and matches the chimney and front steps. Off-white and the blue-green trim color were used to make the once-bland entryway come alive with visual interest. Note how the trim color is painted on the foundation area to tie it in with the rest of the color scheme. "A woman who grew up in our bungalow, her father built it and they moved in when she was four, visited us for the first time. . . . She was thrilled with the paint scheme," comments the owner.

Alternate Color Schemes

Body: Rookwood Blue Green
Major trim: Classical White
Window sash: Canyon Clay
Accents: Birdseye Maple

Body: Downing Stone
Major trim: Dried Thyme
Window sash: Ethereal White
Accents: Ivorie

OWENS BUNGALOW

San Diego, California

Body: Colonial Revival Stone

Major trim: Rookwood
   Medium Brown

Window sash: Polished
   Mahogany

Accents: Rookwood Terra Cotta

Original Colors:

Typical of many modern-colored bungalows is white trim against a brown body. This is a simple but less effective scheme.

Desired Look:

To enliven the front façade and add some pizzazz. To have the house look "more natural—to emerge from the site."

New Colors:

By changing the colors of the body to a lighter stone color and darkening the trim, a softer, more natural Arts & Crafts feel is achieved. Terra-cotta was added to highlight the porch features. Paint was removed from the chimney and porch piers to return them to their original condition. The house now has a special sense of place.

Alternate Color Schemes

Body: Harvester
Major trim: Roycroft Vellum
Window sash: Domino
Accents: Quartersawn Oak

Body: Coastal Plain
Major trim: Alpaca
Window sash: Rookwood Dark Red
Accents: Rare Gray

Tomita/Berkowitz Craftsman

San Diego, California

Body, stucco: Birdseye Maple

Body, shingles: Butternut

Major Trim: Craftsman Brown

Minor trim/window sash:
   Rookwood Dark Red

Original Colors:

A lack of contrast between the floors is increased by the red trim color. The front porch wall is colored so dark that it nearly disappears. The use of a heavy brown trim color obscures details such as rafter ends.

Desired Look:

To bring each surface material into clearer focus, to soften the lower floor, and to reduce the contrast between the window trim color and the rest of the color scheme.

New Colors:

Red-over-clay and sand-over-brown color schemes were first considered and rejected. A much lighter color (butternut) was chosen for the upper floor and a darker one (a Craftsman-era brown) for the lower level. A medium accent color that complemented both floors was selected to highlight the many diverse elements of the house. The window trim was softened to allow the true colors of the body to come forward. Note: This house received the San Diego Preservation Society's Save Our Heritage Organization award.

Alternate Color Schemes

Body, stucco: Renwick Golden Oak
Body, shingles: Restrained Gold
Major trim: Antique White
Minor trim/window sash: Eclipse

Body, stucco: Moroccan Brown
Body, shingles: Svelte Sage
Major trim: Reticence
Minor trim/window sash: Tricorn Black

Reinhardt Bungalow

East Lansing, Michigan

Body: Rookwood Dark Green

Trim: Downing Earth

Window sash: Polished Mahogany

Original Colors:

This yellow-and-white scheme is attractive but lacks any great visual interest. The white sash blends into the trim boards, and the chimney stands starkly against the softer colors of the house.

Desired Look:

A darker body with a lighter trim and a supplemental color. The owners wanted a "spiffy and special look, something that stood out, with an Arts & Crafts–compatible set of colors."

New Colors:

Once color testing was underway, it became clear that a very light trim was not preferred. By bringing all the colors into a closer natural harmony, the house seems less neutral. An earth color was selected for the body and a dark green for the trim. Darkening the window sash to a deep mahogany helped to highlight the trim boards. The darker trim color better outlines the house. The owners feel the house now presents a "very pleasing effect."

Alternate Color Schemes

Body: Yam
Trim: Alabaster
Window sash: Coconut Husk
Accents: Hopsack

Body: Rosemary
Trim: Jersey Cream
Window sash: Terra Brun
Accents: Anjou Pear

FANDEL FOURSQUARE

Seattle, Washington

Body: Rookwood Dark Green

Major trim: Sand

Window Sash: Rookwood Red

Accents: Rookwood Clay

Original Colors:

This home, designed by Seattle architect V. W. Voorhees in 1906, was colored to reflect the light soft pastels of the Victorian revival. A pink body and blue trim don't allow the Arts & Crafts features in this home to be appreciated.

Desired Look:

"Elegant" and "understated" were the key words in developing this paint scheme, something that would work well in the overcast conditions of the Northwest.

New Colors:

Dramatically changing the body color from light to dark instantly alters the look of the house. The red window sash and the vellum trim help the distinctive corner-oriel windows to be accentuated. The eaves brackets are highlighted, as they provide an attractive cap to the overall design. This color scheme is a classic, drawn from the pages of an early-twentieth-century paint brochure.

Alternate Color Schemes

Body: Craftsman Brown
Major trim: Navajo White
Window sash: Roycroft Bronze Green
Accents: Sage

Body: Blonde
Trim: Renwick Golden Oak
Window sash: Fireweed
Accents: Roycroft Vellum

STEARNS CRAFTSMAN

Portland, Oregon

Body: Bunglehouse Gray

Major trim: Roycroft
    Bronze Green

Accents: Roycroft Vellum

Original Colors:

This wonderful Arts & Crafts home suffers from the all-too-common "over-contrast" color scheme of very dark brown body and very light trim. The fact that the house was in a rough stucco was lost in the heavy body color.

Desired Look:

The centerpiece of a new development, the house needed to look attractive, classy, and historical in nature.

New Colors:

A dramatic change in body color, from dark to light, helps the house fit in not only with its historic neighbors but with the new development as well. The rough Arts & Crafts stucco work can now be seen clearly.

Alternate Color Schemes

Body: Softer Tan
Major trim: Quiver Tan
Window sash: Rookwood Dark Red
Accents: Birdseye Maple

Body: Sage
Major trim: Mocha
Window sash: Black Bean
Accents: Roycroft Vellum

MOSLEY BUNGALOW

Atlanta, Georgia

Body: Bunglehouse Gray

Major trim: Stepping Stone

Window sash: Rookwood Dark Red

Accents: Niagara Mist

Original Colors:

Lost in a sea of light colors under a heavy gray roof, this bungalow seems dropped from out of nowhere onto the landscape.

Desired Look:

The Arts & Crafts philosophy calls for natural colors and tones that help the house nestle into its surroundings.

New Colors:

A green-gray body color sets the background for a darker gray trim. A dark red was chosen for the windows and front door. The roof now seems part of the overall plan and is better complemented by the house colors.

Alternate Color Schemes

Body: Oakmoss
Major trim: Ionic Ivory
Window sash: Superior Bronze
Accents: Clary Sage

Body: Ancestral Gold
Major trim: Dapper Tan
Window sash: Polished Mahogany
Accents: Mannered Gold

MILLER BUNGALOW

Auburn, Washington

Body: Biltmore Bluff

Major trim: Willowbrook

Minor trim: Roycroft Vellum

Window sash: Rookwood Red

Accents: April Shower

Original Colors:

The light blue body and white trim provides a cottage look to this pyramid-roofed bungalow. While pleasant enough, the house looks rather Colonial.

Desired Look:

The original conception was to continue with a blue body and just change the trims and accents.

New Colors:

After some color testing, it was decided to switch to a more traditional bungalow scheme with a yellow-buff body and soft-green trim. The house now takes on a period look. The addition of dark red windows and soft blue accents provides a pleasant combination. "The house looks great! Everyone loves it!" remarks the owner.

Alternate Color Schemes

Body: Camelback
Trim: Birdseye Maple
Window sash: Rookwood Dark Red
Accents: Rookwood Dark Green

Body: Hammered Silver
Trim: Griffin
Window sash: Polished Mahogany
Accents: Ivorie

LeCraft Bungalow

Miles City, Montana

Body: Bunglehouse Gray

Major trim: Sage Green Light

Accents: Rookwood Red

Original Colors:

Painted in two shades of blue, this classic front-gabled bungalow from 1914 seems out of context with its surroundings.

Desired Look:

A period scheme was desired to radically shift the look of the house away from a cute cottage to an Arts & Crafts–period example. The owner wanted the warm glow that only a bungalow can emit. Originally, gray, light green, and even white were considered, but all were rejected as not having enough substance.

New Colors:

A medium to light body in a gray-green is framed by a trim in a darker shade of the same color. Highlights such as roof rafters and doors are painted in a historic red, giving the little bungalow a great deal of character. In testing the colors, the owner involved the neighbors. "Before my house was blue, it was awful pink. Just imagine being the neighbors who had to look at those colors for such a long time and in succession. My neighbors see the house more than I do, so I thought it fitting to heed their advice."

Alternate Color Schemes

Body: Sage
Major trim: Anonymous
Window sash: Roycroft Bronze Green
Accents: Birdseye Maple

Body: Weathered Shingle
Major trim: Roycroft Vellum
Window sash: Garden Gate
Accents: Whole Wheat

BOWIE BUNGALOW

Orange, California

Body: Bunglehouse Gray

Major trim: Roycroft Vellum

Window sash: Roycroft Bottle
    Green

Accents: Downing Straw

Original Colors:

In the 1970s and 1980s, many bungalows were painted to look like quaint cottages. This pyramid bungalow is colored in a blue body with white trim.

Desired Look:

A return to historic Arts & Crafts–style colors and color placement.

New Colors:

The stark white trim was softened by changing it to vellum, and the blue body was covered in a green-gray popularly shown in a 1916 Sears Roebuck and Co. paint catalog. The windows, formerly rose, are now painted in dark green, which is more in keeping with historic period examples. The roof rafters, previously ignored, are now highlighted in a medium yellow.

Alternate Color Schemes

Body: Birdseye Maple
Major trim: Rookwood Brown
Window sash: Roycroft Bronze Green
Accents: Rookwood Terra Cotta

Body: Eminent Bronze
Major trim: Roycroft Suede
Window sash: Domino
Accents: Roycroft Copper Red

ROMARY BUNGALOW

Lawrence, Kansas

Body: Sage

Gables and bays: Audubon Green

Trim: Birdseye Maple

Window sash: Rookwood Red

Accents: Roycroft Vellum and
Rookwood Dark Green

Porch floor: Rookwood Dark
Green

Original Colors:

Beginning in the 1930s, bungalows such as this front-gabled type were simply colored with an all-white scheme. Easy to maintain, this monochromatic scheme was repainted many times.

Desired Look:

Multiple colors to help frame the house and to highlight the architectural elements.

New Colors:

The medium yellow trim provides a strong outline for this transformed bungalow. Sage, suede, and some browns were tested before settling on a medium-green body. Deep-red window sash and dark-green accents help transform this home from bland to exciting. In the end, a total of five colors was employed on the house. The use of green tones helps the house fit snugly into the landscape, as suggested by Arts & Crafts–period designers. During the painting, passersby complemented the owner about the dramatic color shift and were quite impressed with the overall change.

Alternate Color Schemes

Body: Portabello
Trim: Interactive Cream
Window sash: Rookwood Dark Green
Accents: Roycroft Vellum

Body: Reddish Earth
Trim: Panda White
Window sash: Quiver Tan
Accents: Restrained Gold

DUPREY BUNGALOW

Ann Arbor, Michigan

Body top: Rookwood Dark Brown

Body bottom: Craftsman Brown

Trim: Roycroft Vellum

Accents: Rookwood Terra Cotta

Original Colors:

This bungalow is covered in white vinyl siding and has had many of its decorative features removed.

Desired Look:

Restoration of the porch and eaves brackets, and colors more appropriate to the era in which it was constructed.

New Colors:

The upper floors are in a dark-brown shingle over a lighter tan lower section. The trim is a dark green and the windows are white. Dramatic color is added by employing terracotta on the rebuilt porch columns and eaves brackets.

Alternate Color Schemes

Body top: Aurora Brown
Body bottom: Birdseye Maple
Trim: Roycroft Vellum
Window sash: Andiron
Accents: Sage

Body top: Downing Sand
Body bottom: Rookwood Dark Green
Trim: Virtual Taupe
Window sash: Roycroft Vellum
Accents: Birdseye Maple

CORPORATION FOR ENVIRONMENTAL MANAGEMENT OFFICES FOURSQUARE

Indianapolis, Indiana

Body: Bunglehouse Gray

Trim: Roycroft Bronze Green

Bay and dormers: Birdseye Maple

Accents: Paris White

Original Colors:

Shown here during its renovation into an office building in a historic redevelopment area, this Arts & Crafts Foursquare was once white with blue trim.

Desired Look:

An extensive interior renovation spurred the desire for an equally stunning exterior. "With the inside unbelievably beautiful—we would like the outside to look just spectacular," commented the owner. The colors also needed to harmonize with the new charcoal-gray roof.

New Colors:

A darker bronze trim helps frame the building and allows for a medium gray body to appear lighter against it. The combination provides a solid look to the structure. Maple is employed as an accent color on the roof dormers and other decorative panels, and off-white was used for the details. The addition of the maple gave an extra punch to the details. The outcome was classy and sophisticated.

Alternate Color Schemes

Body: Well-Bred Brown
Trim: Lucent Yellow
Window sash: Rookwood Dark Red
Bay and dormers: Portabello
Accents: Roycroft Bronze Green

Body: Renwick Olive
Trim: Dover White
Window sash: Fiery Brown
Bay and dormers: Butternut
Accents: Ecru

Engler Bungalow

Liverpool, New York

Body: Roycroft Suede

Trim: Yuma Green

Window sash: Rookwood Red

Accents: Gazebo White

Original Colors:

This lovely double-gable-front bungalow is lost in a bland sea of white paint. No architectural features stand out. Try to pick out five features of the house you would highlight.

Desired Look:

The owner wanted period colors and the correct tones on the house. "I've seen some disastrous uses of dark green that probably looked fine in a two-by-two-inch paint sample, but when painted on a house, look overly saturated. At one point I had seen a house that was pumpkin colored, with taupe, and a moss green accent. When I tried to match paint samples, everything looked like bright orange!"

New Colors:

Totally repainted in a soft suede body with dark gray-green trim, the house takes on new life. The window sash, now in a period red, stand out from the trim, as does the first gable now that the divider is colored in a contrasting tone.

Alternate Color Schemes

Body: Tatami Tan
Trim: Antique White
Window sash: Polished Mahogany
Accents: Hardware

Body: Sensible Hue
Trim: Mocha
Window sash: Best Bronze
Accents: Antique White

McCusker Craftsman

West Hartford, Connecticut

Body: Birdseye Maple

Trim: Audubon Green

Window sash: Oxford Ivy

Accents: Gazebo White and
    Rookwood Brown

Original Colors:

This handsome Craftsman-style home is painted in gray with white trim and is nothing special. Everything seems colored in one light tone.

Desired Look:

"We would like historical colors or at least historically appropriate colors. We would like it to be eye-catching . . . and pleasing to our tastes. Can we have it all?" the owner asked.

New Colors:

Entirely recolored in a maple body with medium green trim, the house reflects the age of Stickley. The window sash is now in a period dark green with just enough contrast to stand out from the trim. Accents in off-white and a period brown help features on the porches to become prominent. The porch columns are now much more noticeable.

Alternate Color Schemes

Body: Oakmoss
Trim: Natural Choice
Window sash: Domino
Accents: Mindful Gray and Ivorie

Body: Butterscotch
Trim: Rookwood Dark Green
Window sash: Polished Mahogany
Accents: Roycroft Vellum and
Renwick Olive

IT WAS PURELY USEFUL, AND SIMPLY BEAUTIFUL. *But the Arts & Crafts Movement was more than California bungalows and Prairie School villas. It was a blend of Victorian windows, Queen Anne sash, Colonial columns, Gothic half-timbering, Mission dormers and bungalow brackets—all painted in the deep, rich Roycroft colors. And whether you're a craftsman purist, or you just like the look, our Preservation Palette® has all the colors you need for utilitarian beauty.*

These color palettes, provided by Sherwin-Williams, feature many of the colors suggested on the previous pages and are a good resource to help you begin to select colors for your home.

Arts & Crafts color palette and color swatches on pages 151—183 reprinted courtesy of Sherwin-Williams. ©2002 The Sherwin-Williams Company. All rights reserved.

Roycroft Vellum
SW 2833

Birdseye Maple
SW 2834

Craftsman Brown
SW 2835   P1

Quartersawn Oak
SW 2836

Hammered Silver
SW 2840

Roycroft Copper Red
SW 2839

Polished Mahogany
SW 2838

Aurora Brown
SW 2837

Roycroft Mist Gray
SW 2844

Roycroft Brass
SW 2843

Roycroft Suede
SW 2842

Weathered Shingle
SW 2841

Bunglehouse Gray
SW 2845

Roycroft Bronze Green
SW 2846

Roycroft Bottle Green
SW 2847

Roycroft Pewter
SW 2848

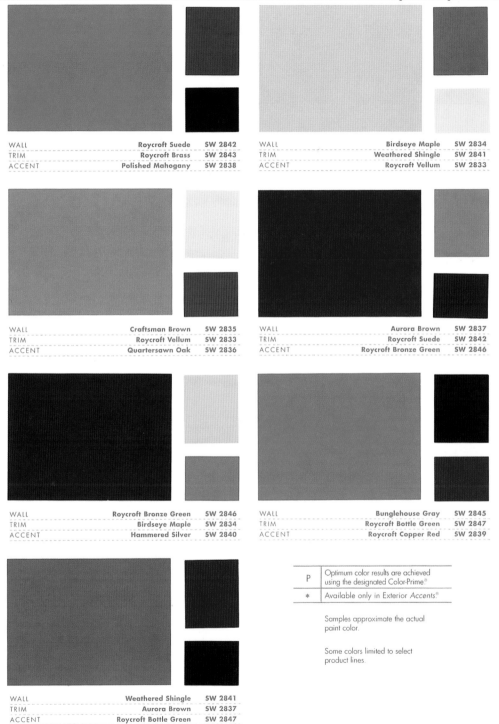

WALL	Roycroft Suede	SW 2842
TRIM	Roycroft Brass	SW 2843
ACCENT	Polished Mahogany	SW 2838

WALL	Birdseye Maple	SW 2834
TRIM	Weathered Shingle	SW 2841
ACCENT	Roycroft Vellum	SW 2833

WALL	Craftsman Brown	SW 2835
TRIM	Roycroft Vellum	SW 2833
ACCENT	Quartersawn Oak	SW 2836

WALL	Aurora Brown	SW 2837
TRIM	Roycroft Suede	SW 2842
ACCENT	Roycroft Bronze Green	SW 2846

WALL	Roycroft Bronze Green	SW 2846
TRIM	Birdseye Maple	SW 2834
ACCENT	Hammered Silver	SW 2840

WALL	Bunglehouse Gray	SW 2845
TRIM	Roycroft Bottle Green	SW 2847
ACCENT	Roycroft Copper Red	SW 2839

WALL	Weathered Shingle	SW 2841
TRIM	Aurora Brown	SW 2837
ACCENT	Roycroft Bottle Green	SW 2847

| P | Optimum color results are achieved using the designated Color-Prime® |
| * | Available only in Exterior *Accents*® |

Samples approximate the actual paint color.

Some colors limited to select product lines.

RESOURCES

ROOFING

Ameri-Clay Roof Tile
www.americlay.com

ATAS International Inc.
6612 Snowdrift Road
Allentown, PA 18106
800-468-1441
info@atas.com
www.atas.com
(metal roofing)

Atlas Roofing Corporation
1775 The Exchange, Suite 160
Atlanta, GA 30339
800-251-2852
www.atlasroofing.com

BPB America, Inc.
5301 West Cypress Street
Suite 300
Tampa, FL 33607-1766
866-4 BPB USA
www.bpb-celotex.com

CertainTeed Corporation
P.O. Box 860
750 East Swedesford Road
Valley Forge, PA 19482
610-341-7000
corporate@certainteed.com
www.certainteed.com

Columbia Roof Tile
8650 - 130th Street
Surrey, BC V3W 1G1
Canada
877-388-8453
rooftile@crooftile.com
www.crooftile.com

The Durable Slate Company
1050 North Fourth Street
Columbus, OH 43201
800-666-7445
tile@durableslate.com
www.durableslate.com

Elk Roofing
Elk Corporation of America
14643 Dallas Parkway
Suite 1000
Dallas, TX 75254
866-355-0607
webinfo@elkcorp.com
www.elkcorp.com

Evergreen Slate Company, LLC
68 East Potter Avenue
P.O. Box 248
Granville, NY 12832
518-642-2530
www.evergreenslate.com

GAF Materials Corporation
150 East Anton Drive
Romeoville, IL 60446
815-372-9701
ResidentialSales@gaf.com
www.gaf.com

Georgia-Pacific Corporation
133 Peachtree Street NE
Atlanta, GA 30303
404-652-4000
www.gp.com

IKO
IKO Industries Ltd.
602-1 Yorkdale Road
Toronto, ON M6A 3A1
Canada
sales.help@iko.com
800-433-2811
www.iko.com

Johns Manville
P.O. Box 5108
717 - 17th Street
Denver, CO 80217
800-654-3103
www.jm.com

Meeker Cedar Shakes
Meeker Cedar Products, Ltd.
P.O. Box 381
Sumas, WA 98295
800-663-8761
www.meekercedar.com

Owens Corning
One Owens Corning Parkway
Toledo, OH 43659
800-GET-PINK
www.owens-corning.com

Reinke Shakes Inc.
210 South 4th Street
Hebron, NE 68370
402-365-7521
www.reinkeshakes.com
(metal shingles)

Slate International, Inc.
3422 Old Capitol Trail
Suite 1061
Wilmington, DE 19808
301-952-0120
www.slateinternational.com

Tamko Roofing Products
Tamko Corporation
220 West 4th Street
Joplin, MO 64801
800-641-4691
sales@tamko.com
www.tamko.com

TEAL Cedar Products Ltd.
17897 Trigg Road
Surrey, BC V4N 4M8
Canada
888-995-TEAL
sales@tealcedar.com
www.tealcedar.com

Paints & Stains

Behr Process Corporation
3400 West Segerstrom Avenue
Santa Ana, CA 92704
800-854-0133
www.behrpaint.com

Benjamin Moore & Company
51 Chestnut Ridge Road
Montvale, NJ 07645
800-826-2623
www.benjaminmoore.com

Cabot Wood Care Products
100 Hale Street
Newburyport, MA 01950
800-US-STAIN
www.cabotstain.com

Color Guild International
3090 South Jamaica Court
Suite 100
Aurora, CO 80014
800-995-8885
www.colorguild.com

Devoe Paint Company
925 Euclid Avenue
Cleveland, OH 44115-1487
800-454-3336
devoepaint@ici.com
www.devoepaint.com

Dunn-Edwards
4885 East 52nd Place
Los Angeles, CA 90040
800-537-4098
888-DE-PAINT
www.dunnedwards.com

Dutch Boy/Cuprinol
101 Prospect Avenue
Cleveland, OH 44115
800-828-5669
www.dutchboy.com

Fine Paints of Europe
P.O. Box 419
Woodstock, VT 05091
800-332-1556
info@finepaints.com
www.finepaints.com

Fuller O'Brien
925 Euclid Avenue
Cleveland, OH 44115-1487
866-931-1955
www.fullerpaint.com

The Glidden Company
925 Euclid Avenue
Cleveland, OH 44115
800-GLIDDEN (454-3336)
www.gliddenpaint.com

ICI Dulux Paint Centers
925 Euclid Avenue
Cleveland, OH 44115-1487
800-984-5444
www.iciduluxpaints.com

Martin Senour Paints
101 Prospect Avenue NW
1500 Midland Building
Cleveland, OH 44115
800-677-5270
www.martinsenour.com

Old Village Paint
P.O. Box 1030
Fort Washington, PA
  19034-1030
610-238-9001
info@old-village.com
www.old-village.com

Olde Century Colors
24656 Old Cleveland Road
South Bend, IN 46628
800-222-3092
Barb@OldeCenturyColors.com
www.oldecenturycolors.com

Olympic
One PPG Place
Pittsburgh, PA 15272
www.olympic.com

Pittsburgh Paints
One PPG Place
Pittsburgh, PA 15272
800-441-9695
www.pittsburghpaints.com

Pratt & Lambert Specialty Products
P.O. Box 1505
Buffalo, NY 14240
800-289-7728

Sherwin-Williams Company
101 Prospect Avenue
Cleveland, OH 44115
800-336-1110
www.sherwin.com

Valspar
Headquarters in
Minneapolis, MN
800-323-8418
Architectural Customer Service
1191 Wheeling Road
Wheeling, IL 60090
800-845-9061
www.valspar.com

HISTORICAL MUSEUMS & HISTORIC SITES

Craftsman Farms
2352 Route 10 West, #5
Morris Plains, NJ 07950
973-540-1165
www.parsippany.net/
craftsmanfarms.html

The Foundation for the Study of the Arts & Crafts Movement at Roycroft
31 South Grove Street
East Aurora, NY 14052
716-652-3333
info@roycroftshops.com
www.roycroft.org

Frank Lloyd Wright Preservation Trust
951 Chicago Avenue
Oak Park, IL 60302
708-848-1976
www.wrightplus.org
(home and studio)

The Gamble House
4 Westmoreland Place
Pasadena, CA 91103
626-793-3334
www.gamblehouse.org

The Lanterman House
4420 Encinas Avenue
La Cañada–Flintridge, CA 91012
818-790-1421

Marston House
An Arts & Crafts Mansion
3525 Seventh Avenue
Balboa Park
San Diego, CA 92103
619-298-3142
858-292-0455

The Percell-Cutts House
2328 Lake Place
Minneapolis, MN 55405
612-870-3131

Pewabic Pottery
10125 East Jefferson Avenue
Detroit, MI 48214
313-822-0954
www.pewabic.com

The Pleasant House
217 South Home Avenue
Oak Park, IL 60302
708-383-2654

Riordan Mansion
409 Riordan Road
Flagstaff, AZ 86001
www.pr.state.az.us/parkhtml/
  riordan.html

ORGANIZATIONS

Advisory Council on Historic Preservation
1100 Pennsylvania Avenue NW
Suite 809
Old Post Office Building
Washington, DC 20004
202-606-8503
achp@achp.gov
www.achp.gov

The Association for Preservation Technology
4513 Lincoln Avenue
Suite 213
Lisle, IL 60532-1290
630-968-6400
information@apti.org
www.apti.org

Friends of Terra Cotta
771 West End Avenue
Suite 10E
New York, NY 10025
212-932-1750
www.preserve.org/fotc

Historic Chicago Bungalow Initiative
www.chicagobungalow.org

National Register of Historic Places
National Park Service
1849 C Street NW
NC400
Washington, DC 20240
202-343-9536
202-343-9500
nr_info@nps.gov
www.cr.nps.gov/nr/

National Trust for Historic Preservation
1785 Massachusetts Avenue NW
Washington, DC 20036
202-588-6000
www.nationaltrust.org

Preservation Action
1350 Connecticut Avenue NW
Suite 401
Washington, DC 20036
202-659-0915
mail@preservationaction.org
www.preservationaction.org

The Rohm and Haas Paint Quality Institute
www.paintquality.com
(comprehensive educational resource for homeowners, painting professionals, and paint sellers)

State Historic Preservation Offices
www.sso.org/ncshpo/shpolist.htm

Twin Cities Bungalow Club
www.mtn.org/bungalow

William Morris Society
www.morrissociety.org

PERIODICALS

American Bungalow
123 South Baldwin Avenue
Sierra Madre, CA 91024
800-350-3363
www.ambungalow.com

Fine Homebuilding
The Taunton Press
63 South Main Street
P.O. Box 5506
Newton, CT 06470
203-426-8171
www.finehomebuilding.com

Old House Journal
2 Main Street
Gloucester, MA 01930
978-283-3200
www.oldhousejournal.com

Period Homes
69A Seventh Avenue
Brooklyn, NY 11217
718-636-0788
www.period-homes.com

Style 1900
333 North Main Street
Lambertville, NJ 08530
609-397-4104

This Old House Magazine
1185 Avenue of the Americas
New York, NY 10036
800-898-7237
www.thisoldhouse.org

Traditional Building Magazine
69A Seventh Avenue
Brooklyn, NY 11217
718-636-0788
www.traditional-building.com

Victorian Homes
Y-Visionary Publishing
265 South Anita Drive
Suite 120
Orange, CA 92868
714-939-9991
www.victorianhomesmag.com

RESTORATION ASSISTANCE

The Bungalow Gutter Bracket Company
P.O. Box 22144
Lexington, KY 40522
859-335-1555
www.bungalowgutterbracket.com

Craftsman Hardware Company, Ltd.
P.O. Box 161
Marceline, MO 64658
660-376-2481

Historic Exterior Color Consulting
Robert Schweitzer
3661 Waldenwood Drive
Ann Arbor, MI 48105
734-668-0298
www.arts-crafts.com/market/robs

Rocheford Handmade Tile
3315 Garfield Avenue South
Minneapolis, MN 55408
612-824-6216
www.housenumbertiles.com
(ceramic-tile house numbers)

WEB SITES

The Arts & Crafts Society
www.arts-crafts.com

Bob Vila's Home Site
info@bobvila.com
www.bobvila.com

The Craftsman Homes Connection
www.crafthome.com

HGTV (Home & Garden Television)
www.hgtv.com

Home Depot
www.homedepot.com

Lowe's
www.lowes.com

Pasadena Heritage
www.pasadenaheritage.org

Restoration Central
www.restorationcentral.com

This Old House
www.thisoldhouse.org

World of Old Houses
www.oldhouses.com.au

EXTERIOR PAINT PROBLEM ANSWERS

www.architecture.about.com/
library/bl-preservationbrief
paint.htm

www.doityourself.com/paint/
extprob.htm

www.forestry.iastate.edu/ext/
repaint.html

www.lowes.com

www.oldhouseweb.com/
stories/How-To/Paints/

www.paintquality.com

NEW BUNGALOW PLANS

The Bungalow Company
P.O. Box 584
550 SW Industrial Way
Suite 37
Bend, OR 97702
888-945-9206
541-312-2674
www.thebungalowcompany.com

Princeton Plans Press
Craftsman Homes
P.O. Box 622
Princeton, NJ 08540
800-566-9655
www.pplans.com

COLOR WHEELS

The Color Wheel Company
P.O. Box 130
Philomath, OR 97370-0130
541-929-7526
info@colorwheelco.com
www.colorwheelco.com

BIBLIOGRAPHY

Armstrong, Tim. *Colour Perception: A Practical Approach to Colour Theory.* Jersey City, NJ: Parkwest Publications, 1993.

Cigliano, Jan, and Walter Smalling. *Bungalow: American Restoration Style.* Salt Lake City, UT: Gibbs Smith, Publisher, 1998.

Clark, Robert Judson. *The Arts and Crafts Movement in America: 1876–1916.* Princeton, NJ: Princeton University Press, 1992.

Cumming, Elizabeth, and Wendy Kaplan. *Arts and Crafts Movement.* New York: Thames and Hudson, 1991.

Duchscherer, Paul, and Douglas Keister. *The Bungalow: America's Arts and Crafts Home.* New York: Penguin, 1996.

Itten, Johannes. *The Art of Color: The Subjective Experience and Objective Rationale of Color.* New York: John Wiley & Sons, 1997.

Kobayashi, Shigenobu. *A Book of Colors: Matching Colors, Combining Colors, Color Designing, Color Decorating.* New York: Kodansha International, 1987.

Lancaster, Clay. *The American Bungalow: 1880–1930.* New York: Abbeville Press, 1985.

Lethaby, William Richard, et al. *Arts and Crafts Houses 1.* London: Phaidon Press, 1999.

Makinson, Randell L. *Greene & Greene: Architecture as a Fine Art.* Salt Lake City, UT: Gibbs Smith, Publisher, 1977.

Makinson, Randell L. *Greene & Greene: The Passion and the Legacy.* Salt Lake City, UT: Gibbs Smith, Publisher, 1998.

McAlester, Virginia, and Lee McAlester. *A Field Guide to American Houses.* New York: Alfred A. Knopf, 2000.

Moss, Roger, ed. *Paint in America.* Washington, DC: National Trust Press, 1996.

Radford Architectural Company. *Radford's Artistic Bungalows.* Chicago: Radford Architectural Company, 1908; Mineola, NY: Dover Publications, 1997.

Schweitzer, Robert, and Michael W. R. Davis. *America's Favorite Homes.* Detroit: Wayne State University Press, 1990.

Sears Roebuck Catalog of Houses. Reprint. Mineola, NY: Dover Publications, 1991.

Smith, Henry Atterbury. *500 Small Houses of the Twenties.* 1923. Reprint, Mineola, NY: Dover Publications, 1990.

Stevenson, Katherine, and H. Ward Jandl. *Houses by Mail.* Washington, DC: The Preservation Press, 1986.

Stickley, Gustav, ed. *Craftsman Bungalows: 59 Homes from* The Craftsman. Mineola, NY: Dover Publications, 1989.

———. *More Craftsman Homes.* Mineola, NY: Dover Publications, 1982.

Turgeon, Kitty, and Robert Rust. *Arts and Crafts (Architecture and Design Library).* New York: Friedman/Fairfax Publishing, 1997.

Vertikoff, Alexander, and Robert Winter. *American Bungalow Style.* New York: Simon & Schuster, 1996.

Winter, Robert. *California Bungalow.* Los Angeles: Hennessey & Ingalls, 1980.